Your Child's Religion

Your Child's Religion

Randolph Crump Miller

HAWTHORN BOOKS, INC.

W. Clement Stone, Publisher

NEW YORK

YOUR CHILD'S RELIGION

Library of Congress Catalog Card Number: 75-5034
ISBN: 0-8015-9118-X

1 2 3 4 5 6 7 8 9 10

Published by arrangement with Doubleday & Company, Inc.

To Phyllis

Preface

1. For whom was this book written?

If you are a parent who is concerned about the spiritual welfare of your children, this book is for you. If you know where to turn for help with physical and emotional problems, but are not sure where to seek religious guidance, this book is for you.

Most parents (and you may be one of them) are certain that religious training is good for their children, but many of them have doubts about the kind of instruction offered in today's churches and schools. You may realize that you are responsible for this religious nurturing process, but you may not be sure of what to do about it. Or you have already tried various means which have failed, and you would like to start again.

Perhaps you have not realized that today we have adequate knowledge concerning the religious development of children and adults. We know that in the relationships of the home are developed the attitudes, responses, motivations, and perspectives which are essential to present and future religious growth. We know that the support of the church as a believing community is significant for the continuing devotion of parents and their children.

This book presents some of this information within the framework of many of the questions parents ask: "How does religion keep my child from becoming a delinquent?" "How do I pick a good Sunday School?" "Why do parents have to

go to Sunday School with their children?" "What do parents
need to do in the home?" "Will religious faith protect my
child from fear and anxiety?"

Parents with very young children will find questions suited
to their needs. Parents with several children will find other
questions which will interest them. Parents of teenagers will
find information about youth groups and the religion of adolescents. There is even one chapter dealing with questions parents
may ask about themselves. Included also is a list of recommended books for use in the home by parents and their children.

Acknowledgments

Grateful acknowledgment is made to the following for permission to reproduce extracts from copyright material in this book:

The American Baptist Publication Society: from *Herein Is Love* by Reuel L. Howe, copyright 1961 by the Judson Press, Valley Forge, Pa. Reproduced by permission.

Cambridge University Press and Oxford University Press: from *The New English Bible*, © The Delegates of the Oxford University Press and the Syndics of the Cambridge University Press 1961.

David McKay Co., Inc.: from *Background to Marriage* by Anne Proctor.

Harper & Brothers: from *The Apostolic Fathers* by Edgar J. Goodspeed and from *The Mystery of Love and Marriage* by D. S. Bailey.

The Macmillan Co.: from *The New Testament in Modern English*, © J. B. Phillips 1958 and from *Jesus of Nazareth* by Joseph Klausner. Used by permission of The Macmillan Co.

Morehouse-Barlow Co., Inc.: from *The Christian Family* by Thomas Van B. Barrett.

Rand McNally & Co.: from *Tell Me about God* by Mary Alice Jones.

The Seabury Press: from *Religion and the Growing Mind* by Basil Yeaxlee.

Thomas Nelson & Sons: from *The Revised Standard Version of the Bible* copyrighted 1946 and 1952 by the Division of Christian Education of the National Council of Churches, and used by permission.

The University of Chicago Press: from *The Complete Bible: an American Translation*, Psalm 103:13, Matthew 7:11, Philippians 2:5 by J. M. Powers Smith and Edgar J. Goodspeed, copyright 1939 by the University of Chicago Press.

University of London Press Ltd.: from *Growing Up in a Modern Society* by Marjorie Reeves.

Students in my class on *Church and Family* at the Yale Divinity School assisted in formulating the questions. Some of the material, rewritten and abridged, appeared in articles in *Children's Religion, The International Journal of Religious Education, The Presbyterian Survey, The Church School Worker,* and *The Earnest Worker.* Mrs. Stanley Harbison and my wife helped to make this a more readable book.

I have used a number of translations of the Bible, with the following abbreviations:
RSV—*Revised Standard Version.*
G—*The Complete Bible: An American Translation.*
P—*The New Testament in Modern English.*
NEB—*The New English Bible: New Testament.*

R.C.M.

Contents

II. THE RELIGIOUS INTERPRETATION OF SECULAR ACTIVITIES

VI. RELIGION, THE CHURCH, AND YOUTH 89

VII. THE FAMILY AND THE CHURCH 101

Your Child's Religion

CHAPTER I

Basic Problems of Parents and Children

2. *Is it the responsibility of the church or the home to help the child develop spiritually?*

How you answer this question for yourself is important, for it will determine your response to many of the things that are said in this book. The conclusion you reach will affect your children and you and your mate as parents. The evidence for finding a solution comes from your understanding of the process of spiritual development, such as how much depends on inner urges and how much on outer influences. Let us look at what happens to a child.

A child's capacity to respond, not only to things but to persons, not only to words but to actions, not only to material conditions but to the spiritual atmosphere, always depends upon his surroundings. Thus his spiritual development must be influenced by the attitudes, actions, and thoughts of those persons who are nearest to him.

The first few formative years are the parents' responsibility, and the child begins to develop as a total person in relation to his parents. His spiritual growth begins with his faith in his parents, who have complete authority over everything that he does. As time goes on, his faith in his parents changes to faith in his parents' faith, and ultimately, if all goes well, he develops a faith of his own. This process of spiritual development later on involves many people, influences, and institutions.

In the earliest years, the home is primary because no other persons of sufficient significance to influence the child have access to him. In some homes, there are grandparents and older children who may have an influence on the child's development. But what happens in the highly personal relationship of mother and infant in feeding, toilet training, and expressions of tenderness will be crucial for the total development of a child, including his capacity for spiritual insight. The father, as we shall see, also has significance, in spite of the confusion about the father's role in today's family.

At first the church's influence is indirect. The parents need the spiritual resources of the church in order to be able to minister to their children, and therefore the kind of experience they have within a local congregation may make a great difference in terms of their influence on their child. The church is concerned more directly with the child when a pastor takes infant baptism or dedication seriously as the opening of the ministry to the child. However, there is no direct ministry until the child is old enough to attend the nursery program of the church. Until this time, he is primarily influenced through his parents.

There are other influences on the child as he goes beyond the immediate environs of his home, and these have a great deal to do with his emotional reactions to the outside world and therefore with his spiritual development.

We may conclude, then, that both home and church share in the responsibility for the religious development of the child and that through both institutions God is at work providing resources for the child's growth.

3. *Why does the church today stress relationships among persons as part of its program?*

The church believes that an individual becomes a person only by being in community with other persons. A baby is born with potentialities for becoming a person, but none of these potentialities will develop unless he has satisfying relationships.

His own person evolves through communication with other persons. If a child is placed in solitary confinement for a period of years, he will be permanently damaged and no later mental development will occur. For example, a girl was reared by wolves in the early period of her life, and after she had been brought into a human community, her reactions remained identical with those of the animals among whom she had lived. She learned to walk on two legs but always dropped back to all four when she wanted to move fast. She never learned to talk or to eat in a human way. She couldn't even imitate other human beings in a home. We do not know how much she might have developed, because she died within three or four years after she was rescued from the animals.

This indicates that the most important thing about becoming a person is to have sound personal relationships, and these are provided for the baby by the parents. The parents can make mistakes as far as the techniques of child care are concerned, but these need not be serious provided the expression and communication of love are never lost. This is a sociological and psychological observation, but it points to the basic religious insight that God comes to persons through other persons. If parents are the mediators of God to their children, God comes through what we call the language of relationships, even though these relationships may include conflict and even resistance.

In becoming a person, the child must have his basic needs satisfied. This involves love and acceptance, parents who can be depended upon, freedom to grow at his own rate, and some satisfaction of his curiosity and sense of wonder, which can begin as early as he explores his own toes. These needs must be satisfied very early if the child is going to develop into a real person. They correspond to our discernment of God's love, God's righteousness, God's gift of growth, and God's transcendent holiness. Parents become channels of the reality of God in the lives of their children long before any words are possible. There needs to be an "atmosphere in which grace flourishes" in the home, at church, at school, and within the neighborhood, for in such circumstances the child's development is likely to be constant and reasonably serene.

4. How can we provide security for our child so that he will be free from fears and anxiety?

Anxiety, which may express itself in terms of fear or dread or loathing or withdrawal, develops primarily out of unsatisfactory relationships. If a baby habitually has to cry too long for attention to his needs, he may be reduced to a state of such helplessness that the tardy arrival of his mother will not overcome it. If the mother is full of anxieties, of whatever sort, she communicates this to the infant by what seems to be a form of empathy; that is, the child seems to share the mother's uncanny emotion. Dr. Harry Stack Sullivan has written that our first learning is normally a negative reaction to anxiety. This can lead to the difficult situation in which a child would rather not eat because of the anxiety caused by contact with his mother.

This indicates that the child's sense of security is a reflection of the mother's emotional security, and when he develops complete trust in his mother because of her dependable response to his needs, there is likely to be a feeling of security. The baby needs tenderness expressed through physical contact, food, warmth, and cleanliness. As the child develops, new feelings, experiences, and situations are likely to arouse anxiety in him, and in his pre-school experience he needs to be helped to overcome it. This means that when the parents have provided a degree of security within the home, they need to help the child make the transfer from the home to the school, church, and neighborhood environment and to give him the kind of backing that will make it possible for him to face the rough and ready world without retreating into a shell or losing his capacity to appreciate the personal worth of others. The parents can help sometimes in guiding friendships or at least in making it possible for the child to have a chum during the pre-adolescent period and in letting him adapt to the gang spirit later on.

Paul Tillich has described what parents need in order to be able to have anxiety-free relationships with their children. He says that religious faith begins with the realization that "you are accepted, accepted by that which is greater than you, and the name of which you do not know. Do not ask the name now: perhaps you will find it later. Do not try to do anything now: perhaps later you will do much. Do not seek for anything; do not perform anything. Simply accept the fact that you are accepted. This is the experience of grace. Everything is transformed. We are able to hear him as by grace we accept others, who have not accepted themselves or us. Our broken relationships are restored. We may not be better than we were before, but our relationships are transfigured."[1]

5. How can I show love to my child and give him freedom without getting into difficulties?

Love always begins and ends on the note of the personal; it involves a degree of possessiveness, a desire to share, and a willingness to make sacrifices for the other. Because it is basically outgoing and sacrificial in its focus, it is willing to give freedom to the other. One form of this love is acceptance of the other person as he is. The result of this personal relationship is first of all trust. Because the parent loves the child, the child in turn not only loves but trusts the parent.

Reuel L. Howe, in *Herein Is Love,* states the objectives of love thus:

1. When we love someone, we seek to help him develop his sense of autonomy, of a capacity to choose for himself in the light of his ability and responsibility. With very small children there are limited areas of choice, such as the selection of toys or blankets or a teething ring. As the child gets older, he may make decisions about what television program to watch or in what order to do his homework or whether to accept an invitation to a friend's house. As the area of freedom widens, there is more and more conflict, and the purpose of love at this point is to give as much freedom as possible without undue risk.

The child, however, seeking always greater areas of freedom, is likely to go beyond his depth unless restrictive measures are taken; and this is the kind of control that love must provide.

2. Love also seeks to develop in the beloved an increasing sense of initiative, a willingness to make decisions and act on them. This willingness to move ahead with imagination and make choices that have meaning for the individual is a very important aspect in the process of growing up.

3. Love seeks also to develop in the beloved a sense of industry, a willingness to carry through on decisions that have been made. Often this is simply in terms of encouragement, the boosting of morale, but in some cases it involves directive measures in order that desirable outcomes may be obtained. The sense of industry begins with play and moves over into schooling and finally into the area of work. There is a continuity here and much depends upon the motivation in the early years.

4. Love helps a person to develop a sense of identity: an image of his own person. He begins to think of himself as a dumbbell or as competent or as handsome, depending upon the way in which people treat him, and this view tends to remain with him in his later life. Nicknames may be both apt and cruel, reflecting the kind of names American Indians use to describe each other. Parents need to help the child develop an accurate image of himself as one who is loved by his parents and therefore loved by God and therefore assisted in developing competence to be a person. Thus the child will be well prepared for adolescence.

5. Finally, Howe suggests, the child is assisted by his parents' love to develop a sense of integrity, of wholeness, of relationship to some value or person outside himself. This means that he has developed the capacity, as Tillich says, to accept other people as they are and to enter into deep and meaningful personal relationships. We see our young people developing this kind of friendship on a semi-permanent basis both with their own sex and with those of the opposite sex, sometimes by going steady

but always by exploring the personal worth of others of their own age.[2]

Love is able to achieve these objectives by means of the successful guidance of parents. As the child gains more and more freedom, he will, it is hoped, become a whole person.

6. *How can I help my child to be normal and to socialize? Will the church help him to face the world with confidence and courage? Or will it make him a little strange?*

It is difficult to know what one means by "normal." If this term implies that the person is so well adjusted to his society he is able to adapt himself to almost any kind of situation, this certainly is not the end result of religious faith. Nothing is perhaps better adjusted than a contented cow. When a person moves toward spiritual maturity, he becomes able to relate to almost anyone without adopting that person's standards and outlook. He faces the world with confidence and courage, not because he is "other-directed," but because the center of his life is outside himself, in terms of his belief in God. What he receives from this faith is more lasting than anything that can come from pure conformity. In many cases, this does make the person a little "strange," particularly when his standards are opposed to those of the group to which he belongs. This is the price that Christians and Jews have always had to pay for their faith. When we have the integrity and maturity that the Christian faith offers, we expect adjustment on a level higher than our immediate society.

Children and young people often see this more clearly than their parents, for the parents may have been beaten down by the world. On the other hand, some parents find that their children seem extremely susceptible to the non-Christian values around them and therefore are not developing in the direction in which the parents had hoped. Here is where the parents can test their capacity to accept their children as they are, even though they have departed from the standards of the parents. By the time a child is old enough to make decisions on his own, the parents must respect his freedom and integrity in spite of the fact that he may cause them pain and disappointment.

7. *How can I impress a responsible sense of duty on my children?*

If we recognize that responsibility develops slowly and that our children are beset with all kinds of conflicts as they seek to develop their own sense of autonomy, we discover that their willingness to accept responsibility is demonstrated in both negative and positive ways. Children absorb the atmosphere of their surroundings, and in a dependable home where there is freedom and respect on the one hand and responsibility and orderliness on the other, they are more likely to be amenable to accepting responsibility imposed from without. The difficulty is that often the sense of duty as seen by the parents is foreign to anything that the children are willing to accept, and it takes time and patience to assist our children in developing those inner resources that will enable them to respond freely to the sense of duty. It is something that needs to be lived within the home by the parents before the children will ever develop it.

On the other hand, certain regulations make sense to a child. Simple rules are understood at an early age. By the time he is nine or ten years of age, he can interpret the rules of Little League baseball more easily than he can understand the Ten Commandments, but he is willing to accept sets of regulations as binding. It is during this period that he may become a Cub Scout and abide by those rules. But in all of these cases he must be treated as one who is free to choose to bind himself to such a set of laws. He may very well discard these laws as he outgrows this stage or loses interest in playing baseball, whereas the basic regulations of responsible membership in the household and later on of responsible citizenship involve him in the permanent willingness to accept law and order in his life. The sense of duty comes primarily from the roots of responsibility and orderliness in his home.

8. We send our children to church so they can learn to be honest. Why has my little girl started to steal things around the house?

Stealing by a child who has not yet learned about the rights of possession is not something to be disturbed about but only to be corrected in a friendly and loving way. Boys and girls even up to the age of seven or eight may be involved in such situations no matter what kind of teaching they get from home or church. Their sense of morality develops slowly and the temptations often are irresistible. Furthermore, the church, when it teaches by moral example, succeeds only in projecting an ideal of goodness which is so abstract that the child cannot possibly understand it. That is why such a prayer as "Make me a good boy" or the statement "I go to Sunday School to make me good" are normally mouthings of adult ideas that have no meaning for the child.

Character development continues over a long period of time and involves the co-operation of parents, church, school, and neighborhood. It has been discovered that for purposes of character education, the co-operation of church and home is essential. If a child goes to church and this experience is not reinforced by training in the home, he is likely to have the same set of morals as anyone else. Similarly, if a child is reared in a home where certain moral values are taught and does not find reinforcement from the church, it is likely that he will not develop the moral insight that is desired. Dr. Ernest Ligon's Character Research Project has demonstrated over a period of more than twenty-five years that real changes in choosing between right and wrong on the part of children and young people are possible, provided the parents and the church work together in terms of particular decisions over a long enough period of time.[3]

Sometimes stealing of a serious nature may occur. Three little girls from different families stole some doll clothes from a store. When the parents discovered what had happened, they held a conference and agreed upon a course of action. Each of the girls went to the manager of the store and told what she had stolen, and each agreed to earn the money to replace the doll clothes, which also were returned in their used condition. The parents supplied the money for the store, and set up extra jobs whereby the girls could pay the sums to their parents. Not much preaching was necessary, for the parents had acted responsibly in supporting their daughters and in helping them face the manager and make restitution.

9. *Tim's father is an excellent athlete, but Tim isn't doing too well in Little League. Father is a bit disappointed, but he wants Tim to know that he loves him. How can he show his love without being false to his own athletic pride and interest in baseball?*

A father usually hopes that his son will reflect his own interests and abilities or in some cases compensate for his own lack of ability in certain directions. This particular case, however, is an illustration of a much broader problem. It comes back to the fact that parents need to love their child as he is and to encourage him in the light of his own capacities. Tim doesn't need to be a star athlete or an outstanding scholar or a socialite in order to make his parents happy. It is the immaturity of parents that destroys their relationship with their child when such goals are not reached.

Children tend to identify with adults whom they admire. The father's job in this particular case is to help Tim respect those aspects of his own interests which are within Tim's capacity.

The difficulty arises when a really outstanding parent who has above-average capacities in every way has a child who lacks all of these inherent characteristics. It is hard for the father to accept this, and the result is a frustrated father and an almost paralyzed child. This illustrates that we must not expect more of our children than they are capable of, and one of the most important things about love is that when it is really operating it is concerned enough to discover the potentialities that are

actually there rather than those that are imagined. This kind of
realistic appraisal in love makes possible the development of
the full potential of the child.

10. *We, the parents, are both college graduates. We would
naturally like to see our children go to college, but we realize
that not all of them will be interested or intelligent enough to
attend. Can the resources of the church help us to show our
less gifted children that we still love them and do not consider
them outsiders to the circle of college graduates in the family?*

This question indicates a realistic appraisal of the capacities
of the children on the part of the parents, which is the beginning of an answer to the problem. Too often the parents
project on their children unrealistic expectations about college
and therefore are disappointed when the children are unable
to perform at this level. Just as we need to be intelligent
about helping those of our children who are able to go to
college, so we must be intelligent about providing equally
meaningful experiences for those who are not going to college.

Our purpose is to make clear our hope for our children to
make use of their own potential, our desire to treat them equally
in love, and our acceptance of them as they are. This begins
a long time before college is on the horizon.

Many of the decisions made during the high school period
are indicative of what is anticipated. For those who are not
going to college, there may be plans for alternative forms of
training, for some kind of special technical preparation, or
for the early acceptance of a job opportunity. Each family
needs to equalize its financial structure so that the one who
does not go to college is not penalized.

If all through the developing life of the family these attitudes have been communicated to the children, the ones who
do not go to college can share in the joy of those who are
accepted in the colleges of their choice; and this is as it should
be. Equally, the college-related members of the family will re-

joice in the achievements of those who do not go. This is not easy, and in almost every family someone will fail to communicate in this way, but the attempt should be made.

11. *What is the mother's role in her child's religious development?*

Horace Bushnell, a hundred years ago, made it clear that the parents' faith is communicated to the children whether the parents desire this or not. If the parents have no faith, this also will be communicated. The parents' actions more than their words are what the child grasps.

The one who has the chief opportunity of communicating the faith in the home is the mother. She has primary control of the infant and later on makes most of the decisions in the home. When it comes to the actual teaching of religious concepts, the mother has the chance to read stories to the children, to be with them when they begin to say their prayers, and to communicate the kind of love that makes possible religious devotion in later life. The mother's role is indeed crucial.

God makes woman "the joyous mother of children" (Psalm 113:9, RSV). From the moment of the first child's birth she is continuously in a child's world. Her duties and responsibilities are governed primarily by her child's needs. To her vocation as a wife (which she should never forget) is added the vocation of a mother. In the deliverance and rearing of her child, the female is most clearly distinguished from the male; and in this role we see the full glory of the female. "When a woman is in travail she has sorrow, because her hour has come; but when she is delivered of the child, she no longer remembers the anguish, for joy that a child is born into the world" (John 16:21, RSV).

Her training for this role is mostly informal. A young girl begins to learn how to be a mother in her own home. She receives indirect training from her mother, and develops attitudes that determine the nature of her future motherhood. This training is more important than any course in domestic science or child psychology, although such information is help-ful. Readiness for motherhood comes from the mother's own childhood experiences and whatever knowledge she may have picked up on the way. The mother introduces the baby to his five senses, to the world beyond him, to physical contact as an expression of love, to a sense of security that is free from anxiety.

Realization of three facts helps mothers in performing their role: first, the role keeps changing. The child goes through "stages," and the mother needs to keep adapting herself to these new developments. Additional children may arrive as the first one grows older, and the perspectives of both the mother and the children are changed. The mother needs to take stock from time to time and to change her ways of doing things in terms of the needs of her brood.

Second, she needs to realize that her children learn through the experience of relationships. Especially with young children, what we do and feel is more important than what we say. The relationships of the home are primary and what we say is secondary.

Third, she must realize that a sea of non-Christian values surrounds her Christian home. The children' playmates may not go to any church. The committed Christian family is in a minority, and the children must learn to live as Christians in the world.

12. *How can a father contribute to his child's religious development?*

The father's role in modern society is less understood than that of the mother. Once, when I was talking to a group of teenagers in a suburban community about their relations with their parents, I mentioned ways of dealing with their fathers. One girl laughed and said, "My mother decides that. My father never makes any decisions." The other youngsters nodded in agreement.

Yet the father's role is of vital importance in the child's

development as a whole, and particularly in his religious development. Because the father functions in the outside world, he has an objective point of view which the mother does not have. If he will take the time, he can be a teacher, an interpreter of the work-a-day world from the point of view of a Christian. He can be an authority and bring order into the home. He can become a symbol of both justice and love. He can give his children insight into the moral sense, which they will most likely interpret in his terms.

A child's father is the clue to his concept of God. Religion begins in the parent-child relationship, for if the child is to think of God as Father, as he will when he learns the Lord's Prayer, what matters is that his human father should in some sense represent his Father in heaven. Therefore, the kind of human father a child has determines to some extent how he will think of God. This is made clear in a number of biblical illustrations:

> As a father is kind to his children,
> So the LORD is kind to those who revere him.
> (Psalm 103:13, G)

Or, as Jesus said: "So if you, bad as you are, know enough to give your children what is good, how much more surely will your Father in heaven give what is good to those who ask him for it!" (Matt. 7:11, G.)

Especially during his younger days, a child sees his father psychologically as the basis for his belief in the Fatherhood of God. The father must take time to be with his children. He should take part in Christian teaching in the home, and he should go to church with his family.

Father and mother together provide the child's understanding of the filial relationship out of which religious faith develops, but the father has the chief task of making God's Fatherhood acceptable.

The father's relationship with the mother, both as husband

and as father, is crucial in creating the proper atmosphere of Christian home life. The kind of love and affection he expresses as a husband is of the greatest significance. A selfish and demanding man will make his children, especially the boys, think dominance is the masculine role. As a father, he should be involved in his children's lives from the moment of birth. These affectional relationships need to be personal on the deepest possible level, for children who learn from infancy that they can count on their father's love and justice rarely suffer from feelings of insecurity or anxiety.

To perform a father's functions is not always easy. Many men work long hours and some of them have to be away from home for long periods of time; but the unity of the home depends not so much on his constant presence as on the continuing atmosphere of love and devotion.

Some Sunday Schools, aware that a child's father may be an absentee much of the time, have begun to place fathers in the nursery class so that the child may know that there are other fathers. This gives the child an opportunity to generalize within the limitations of his mind, and thus he knows that God as Father is not necessarily like his own daddy. This procedure can be carried through by having single men and women or husbands and wives as co-teachers in all classes.

13. What happens when I fail to love my child?

This is one of the questions parents ask when they are anxious about their responsibilities. Marriage and family life involve people who are imperfect. To expect perfection and utopia in the family is to be unrealistic. This is clear if we take seriously the Christian doctrine of man. The image of God is planted in every person, and this makes it possible for everyone to respond to love with love. However, this image has been defaced, and by his self-will and self-love, man breaks his relationships with his fellow man. In other words, all men are equal, not only in their value to God, but also in their place as sinners. In breaking our relationships with each other, we are also breaking our relationship with God. Therefore, no parent can expect to be perfect, nor can he expect his children to be perfect.

We are concerned with our failure to live up to our own expectations as parents. We are unfair, selfish, domineering, and neglectful of our children's welfare. We sense a contradiction between what we stand for and what we do. Often we are most annoyed when we see behavior patterns in our children which reflect our own most unpleasant ways of acting. Sometimes we go beyond this kind of blame, which we can see as our own responsibility, and, because of the tremendous amount of writing about parental delinquency, we tend to blame ourselves for everything that our children do. At this point we begin to feel that we have totally failed, and in our discouragement we develop extreme anxiety about our children.

This condition is primarily the result of false expectations. The power of the Christian Gospel is not something that makes us virtuous saints living in a family of equally virtuous children, but is a resource for being our best selves, with all of our imperfections, and for having the power to forgive each other in love for the things that we do to each other. It is this element of forgiveness in love, which indicates a giving of ourselves beforehand, that supports us when everything seems to go wrong. When an atmosphere of mutual trust exists, the parents and children seek to be worthy of this trust, but at the same time they know that when they are unworthy, the forgiveness is already offered if they will only accept it. No one can force someone to forgive another; he can only ask for it; but when real love exists, it is offered before it is asked for. This is the healing and redemptive power of God at work in family life.

children could be out of the way when Daddy returns, so that he may have his peace and quiet for a little while before he spends time with them. The important thing to remember is that the children should have some free time with their father and that this should be sufficiently natural and spontaneous to have value for them, and this cannot be achieved if the father resents them and their noise.

It is the resentment of the father who asks this question that is bothersome. He is asking for peace and quiet rather than for any companionship with his children, and resents the fact that he cannot have it. This leads to a feeling of guilt that he finds incompatible with his Christian ideals. If this is the issue, it is perfectly obvious that his wishes and his ideals are incompatible. Perhaps he should re-examine his motives for seeking peace and quiet. Because Christianity includes not only the idealism which gives him a sense of guilt but also the redeeming quality of Christ's love, it should be possible for him to seek reconciliation with his children even when his own fatigue or short-temperedness or selfishness has led him to reject them when they come near him at this time of day. It has been said that some children have learned, concerning their fathers, that you have to "feed the beast" before you can come near him, and children learn to be tolerant even of impatient and tired-out fathers. There must be sufficient time for understanding to develop between the parents and the children so that they may learn to accept the others with their shortcomings, and this may mean that the children must make great allowances for the shortcomings of their parents. It also means that parents as well as children have certain rights and privileges which must be acknowledged.

15. My job demands that we move quite often, and this upsets my children a great deal. Can the church help them to get settled when we move to a new location and prepare them to leave when we must, so that they don't get emotionally upset?

CHAPTER II

The Religious Interpretation
of Secular Activities

14. When I come home from work, I want a little peace and quiet, but instead I find a madhouse, and I lose my temper with the kids. How can a guy who feels that way about his kids be a Christian?

A Christian is subject to all the normal human emotions. Being a Christian, even when this includes a genuine decision and a sincere commitment to the God of Jesus Christ and worshiping him in the church, does not automatically make anyone a saint. It does not overcome the fatigue and short temper which one has at the end of a tiring day at work. The point is that a Christian is more likely to feel guilty when he scolds his children for something that is certainly not their fault. Normally the children are glad to see Daddy when he returns from work and are likely to overwhelm him with juvenile good cheer which they have saved up for him. Yet, owing to the pressures of modern life, Daddy is not ready for this kind of madhouse welcome when his nerves are frayed. What can he do about it?

One approach to this problem is through good organization. The youngsters can be prepared for the fact that Daddy is tired when he comes home from work, and they can be guided in planning accordingly. This could include a greeting to Daddy which he should be able to respond to, but it may also include plans for the children playing quietly during the time it takes Daddy to recover his equilibrium. Or perhaps the

The constant mobility of the American family, especially when this involves the spiral of job promotion and changing levels of living, can be extremely upsetting to both children and adults. A child finds his greatest security in his family relationships, and these are supported by a sense of being at home in a particular house, which in turn is surrounded by schools, playgrounds, and churches. In such an environment the child makes friends, explores human relationships, and develops a degree of social behavior. To be suddenly uprooted from this kind of environment and set down in a new one with a culture reflecting a different part of the country and sometimes a different social class is understandably upsetting for him.

There has always been this problem when women and children have followed their men in the more mobile occupations, but today's organization man finds that he is moved with more abandon than is a professional baseball player. Men in the armed forces have had long periods of separation from their wives and children, and the latter have often followed them from one base to another.

The basic security in the mobile family lies in the satisfying and secure intimacy of family relationships. This can be maintained within the family no matter what the environment may be. If you take a small child to a strange house or to a strange church, his security rests in the fact that he is able to be near his mother or an older brother or sister, and they must remain with him until he can feel secure in this new environment with new people. So it is with families on the move.

Wise parents, knowing this, are able to prepare their children in advance for the move, to build up their expectations of what they will find in the new location, and to help them share the enthusiasm for Daddy's new job. They can promise them that there will be certain similarities in the new environment. The schools will not be much different; a child can continue in the same grade whether he is in California or New York; he can go to a church of the same denomination and therefore with similar customs, where he will feel at home.

It is this latter element that may be extremely important. Younger children will find that in a church that is really doing its job there will be other children with whom they can feel at home. They will find that the worship service speaks of the same God and Jesus. They will find a sense of security with a teacher who loves children. The older youngsters not only will find this same element in the Sunday School, but often will be invited into a youth group where they will very rapidly get acquainted with those of similar interests. In the previous young people's group, they may have had some kind of going-away party or at least recognition of their leaving, and they may have been commended by their minister to a church in the new location. The crucial thing, however, is the guidance of the parents, who should make sure that the children re-establish similar roots in the new locality.

16. Isn't our job simply to help our children adjust to life? And can't we do this without any help from religion?

If it is the will of the parents to help the children adjust to the secular life of our modern society, they can do this without any help whatever from religion. They have all kinds of assistance to help their children become completely oriented to a secular world without God, without the church, and with reliance on a humanistic culture. If parents wish this for their children, they have no need of the church.

The trouble comes when the children begin to discover that our society is not nearly so secular as their parents suspect. Young children, playing in the neighborhood, are going to hear questions about God, about Jesus, about Jesus' mother, about sin and confession, and about a myriad other items of the religious life. Very soon they will discover that some people call themselves Catholics, others Jews, and others Protestants; they are going to bring these questions home to their parents. The completely secularized parent can very well say that all of this is nonsense believed by other people, but this is not going to satisfy the children. In most communities, even in the schools, there are Christmas pageants, the singing of the Christmas carols, and the impact of religion through Scouts, YMCA and YWCA organizations for boys and girls, and in many cases invitations to the church from other children. Parents simply cannot escape from the fact that our life is impregnated with Christian values and Christian assumptions.

But our job is not simply to help our children adjust to life; it is to help them develop resources that will allow them, not to be *conformed* to this world, but to be *transformed*. Thus they will have the basic integrity and wholeness whereby they may face the vicissitudes of this world with courage and freedom from anxiety.

There are some people who are convinced that these basic religious values can be communicated to their children without help from the church or even from the religious concepts that other people have. Parents who believe this must be true to their convictions. However, on the basis of wide experience and observation, it seems to many parents that even with all the resources of religion it is hard enough to assist our children to grow up with the integrity and wholeness that point toward maturity of faith. Because we want this for our children, we need all the resources we can find, including the resources of the church.

17. Is religion really so important? Isn't it just good moral training?

Many people believe that the purpose of religion is to provide good moral training. Parents sometimes tell their children that they are sending them to Sunday School so they can learn how to be good. Moral training is part of religious training, but it needs to be seen as the fruit of this training rather than its main purpose. Calvin wrote that the chief end of man was "to glorify God and enjoy him forever." This is a far cry from saying that the chief end of man is to be good. There are so many values in life that far transcend the simple problem of goodness. Plato, writing in terms of

Greek philosophy, always mentioned the triad of virtues: goodness, beauty, and truth. This immediately broadens the base of living far beyond simple moral values.

The Christian faith has to do with the meaning of the world we live in. It tells us that this is a world in which God is the Creator. It is a world in which God is the Lord of history and in the end God is not mocked. It tells us that God has entered into an agreement with his people and it is at this point that the moral response of the people according to the law is part of the covenant or agreement between God and his people. It is a recognition of the fact that men are unable on their own account to keep the moral law and so seem to be defeated by the forces of evil. They are ultimately convinced that all is vanity or futility, and they face the future without hope. The Christian faith tells us that there is hope, because God loved the world so much that he sent us Jesus Christ, and in Christ God was reconciling the world to himself. The heart of the Christian faith is that God is a God of love, who is willing to forgive his people, and who enters into personal relationships with them. Because God has already acted for our salvation, and this act of God's love does not depend on how good we are, we then seek to be worthy of our calling by obeying what we believe to be God's will. Goodness is not the chief end of religion, but we seek to be good out of thanksgiving because we are loved. We still stand under God's judgment because we fail to do his will, but we also stand under the hope that his forgiving love will grant us eternal life. This in a nutshell is the religious framework of the Christian faith. Parents will wish to spell it out in many different ways, but they will discover that it can be experienced in the Christian home and in the ongoing life of the Christian church.[1]

18. How can I help my child to find God in his daily life? At school or on the playground?

If we believe that God is a living God who works through

interpersonal relationships, then we need to point to God as we discern him at work underneath the surface of events. Every child needs to realize that no one has seen God at any time, but that where love is at work through persons, there God is. The first letter of John states it this way: "Though God has never been seen by any man, God himself dwells in us if we love one another; his love is brought to perfection within us. . . . God is love; he who dwells in love is dwelling in God, and God in him . . . But if a man says 'I love God,' while hating his brother, he is a liar. If he does not love the brother whom he has seen, it cannot be that he loves God whom he has not seen. And indeed this command comes to us from Christ himself: That he who loves God must also love his brother" (I John 4:12, 16b, 20, NEB).

A child finds God in his daily life through the love shown to him by his parents, and he learns to identify this love as God's love as he grows older. At first he knows only that his parents love him. Later on he learns to sing "Jesus loves me, this I know, for the Bible tells me so," and this will have reality for him only as he finds this love in the interrelationships of worship and play stories in the church's nursery or kindergarten. God is at work through this love, even though the child does not know it. We hope that in time he will come to discern this love as God's work.

But God also works through the order of the universe, and the young child begins to discover that hot things will burn, that heavy things will drop, and finally that the stars move in their courses with an ordered regularity. This order of nature, of which the child becomes aware quite early in life, will help him discover the creative love of a God of law. By the time he is in the second grade, he will probably know more about astronomy than his parents do, and it would be well for the parents to relate this knowledge to God's order in the universe.

But God is present not only in interpersonal relationships and in the order of the universe; he is also to be discovered in what to the child and his parents is nothing short of mysterious. There is in each person what Rudolf Otto calls "the sense of the numinous." By this, Otto means experience of the holiness of a mysterious God whom Isaiah discovered in the temple. It is a sense of wonder, of reverence, of awe, even of fear, because one is in the presence of the Lord. In worship, we are like Moses, who took off his shoes because he was standing on holy ground. A little child often senses this in his prayers as he prepares to enter the mysterious realm of sleep. And certainly he senses it in the reassuring love of his parents, which in itself causes him to wonder. As the child grows older, this kind of experience will be transformed into a highly personal sense of God's presence in his life; he will experience this most often in the worship of the church, but also in the privacy of his own room where he may pray to God in secret.

The parents' job is to help the child find God at work in all of these aspects of daily life. In so recognizing his presence, however, the child is likely to discover that not all of God's creatures seek him in the same way, that many of them treat each other in an unfriendly and oftentimes even in a vicious manner, and that even in church not all of them are genuinely devoted to the will of God. This is why we cannot say that all who go to church are good. We know that this isn't so. When we claim it, all we do is drive people away from the church because of our false pretentions. And our responsibility to the child, it seems to me, is to make him aware of this loving God at work in all aspects of life. Our hope is that in time he will be able to discern God beneath the surface of events and commit himself to him in his daily life.

19. How can I teach my child to be good when there is so much bad around him?

The child learns about values from those around him in whom he has confidence. When the child is young, he learns primarily from his parents, but as he grows older, he more and more absorbs the values of his playmates, particularly of his special chums, and finally of the gang he joins. However, his basic perspective remains that of his family throughout the whole period of growing up, and it takes a very strong reaction against his family to make him disown their value system. Parents, furthermore, have a good deal of control over the kinds of values the children are exposed to. When the child is young, the parents can to some degree control the selection of his playmates, supervise his playtime, and even choose his schools.

As the child grows up, he is exposed to different sets of values in every community in which he functions. He may learn to adapt himself successfully to each community, so that he behaves in an acceptable way in that community. He is able to be all things to all men, but instead of doing this, as Paul did, in terms of a basic principle of operation, he has no central standpoint from which to adapt himself to these other communities. Therefore, he becomes what David Riesman calls "other-directed." He has his own private radar, and he is able to adapt himself almost immediately to any change in the emotional or social climate. This is not the mature person operating in terms of his own integrity, but is simply the reflection of a chameleon who changes his color to suit his environment.

Parents can help their child evaluate the activities and responses of others in terms of the home's value system. This needs to include tolerance, the recognition of the right of others to behave in a different way, and at the same time a realistic approach that makes it possible for him to live successfully in the world.

What worries the average parent, however, is that the bad elements in the surroundings will be more effective in determining the child's outlook than whatever home or church or school influences work for good. It is generally agreed that this will happen when the home is not strong enough. But where the home offers security, companionship, parental guidance, and wise balance between freedom and responsibility, we find that we can trust our children to behave in an acceptable way in almost any situation. This trust is gained, not by preaching to the child, but by helping him to make his own decisions as he becomes capable of doing so within the framework of the various possibilities that are open to him. There is enough of a desire to do the right thing in every child so that this can be appealed to if he lives in an environment where love and security are paramount and where he knows he will be forgiven when he makes a mistake or even when he follows his lowest inclinations.

A child may be pressured, for example, to cheat in examinations. The suggestion may come from his classmates, or he may be asked to contribute to the cheating of another. If much emphasis has been placed on good grades as the badge of success, the inner pressure may be too great and the child will succumb. What has been said above about the home influence applies to cheating, in terms of atmosphere and parental practice. A father who brags about cheating on his income tax must not be surprised if his child cheats on an examination.

If your child cheats, or steals, or lies, what he needs most is your help, understanding, and love, so that he may find strength to resist the temptation the next time. Forgiveness, when it is combined with recognition of the situation and the consequences, is a source of strength as the child seeks to fulfill his potentiality as a whole person.

20. How can I prevent my child from telling lies?

At some stages in the child's development, the telling of lies has no moral implications whatever. It is simply his fantasy system working in a perfectly normal way.

There is a wonderful story about Mary McCoy, who, when running in the garden in the twilight, announced that she saw an elephant. All Mother saw was a gnarled and ancient stump. She scolded Mary and told her to go to her room and ask God's forgiveness for telling a lie. A few minutes later Mary returned from her room with a magnificent smile.

"Did you ask God to forgive you for telling a story?" Mother asked.

"Oh yes. God and I had quite a talk. I told him that I was sorry that I had thought I saw an elephant in the garden but it was just an old stump."

"Well?" asked Mother.

Mary smiled. "God said, 'That's quite all right, Miss Mc-Coy. I thought it was an elephant myself.' "[2]

Some parents have enabled their children to understand that if they are caught telling a lie, the consequences will always be unpleasant, whereas if they tell the truth from the very beginning, the consequences will be less painful as far as punishment is concerned, even though they must live with the situation they have created. When the truth is told openly and freely, forgiveness is easy to offer and not too hard to accept, and then parents and children together can work out the consequences of the act that is involved.

When Billy was nine years old, he and his father visited a park in which there was a lake. Billy wandered into an old, abandoned boathouse. It had a stairway, and Billy's curiosity led him to the top. Suddenly, two big boys jumped out at him and asked him what he was doing there. They pointed to an old canoe attached to the wall and accused him of punching a hole in it. Then they grabbed him and dragged him along with them, saying they were going to the police. At this point they met his father, who asked what had happened. The boys accused Billy of damaging the canoe. The father turned to Billy and asked:

"Did you do that?"

"No," Billy replied.

"Turn him loose," said the father. Then he turned to Billy and said, "Billy, as long as you tell me the truth, I can back you to the hilt. But if you lie to me, I won't be able to back you up."

A child who knows his parents are truthful and trustworthy in their dealings with him will want to be as truthful and trustworthy as they are. He may slip from exact truthfulness occasionally, but unless he is hopelessly branded as a liar (and so discouraged from trying any further), he will continue to try to live up to the standards set forth by loved and trusted parents.

21. *How does religion contribute to the mental health of our child?*

Ideally, religion provides a sense of security, freedom from anxiety, a means of overcoming guilt, and direction for life. This condition exists when the parents have a sound set of religious beliefs, a realistic approach to Christian values, and the kind of community life in the home that provides what we call the "atmosphere in which grace flourishes." Horace Bushnell wrote many years ago that "a child should grow up a Christian and never know himself as being anything else." When the child has this experience of growing in favor with God and man, he is assured of a high degree of mental health. When his beliefs are defensible in the modern world, there is very little danger of his mental health being destroyed by the attacks of the non-Christian elements in society.

It is not true, however, that religion always contributes to the mental health of our children; often it merely intensifies the fears and anxieties of childhood. This is what Horace Bushnell was fighting against a century ago when he attacked the revivalists of his time who were willing to consign all unbaptized children to hell. Children would come to church and hear that there was no chance of their going to heaven. The morality of the church in those days was so restrictive that out of it came a basically negative attitude toward life. The concept of guilt was built up to such an extent, without the corresponding preaching of God's forgiving love, that the fundamental religious attitude was one of fear. When this is developed to an extreme degree, we discover either religious fanaticism or a breakdown in mental health.

We cannot settle for just any brand of religion. Jesus taught that the rewards of religious faith are freedom from worry and anxiety, assurance of the love of God the Father, strength from God through worship, and a high sense of integrity because one's life is centered on God. When this kind of faith is practiced in the home, there is little danger to the mental health of all the members of the family.

22. Are there any religious values in play?

Play is one of the most important activities of man. As such, it is always psycho-physical, almost always voluntary, and fulfilling in itself. It is a form of immediate learning for the simple joy of the activity.

The other important thing to remember is that the ability to play increases as one goes up the evolutionary scale. The higher the intelligence, the more complicated are the toys which a child or an adult may use. The connection between work and play is so close that what starts as play can end as work, and vice versa. A little girl may find a great deal of joy in playing house even when it means washing real dishes. A little boy who plays baseball may grow up to become a professional baseball player. It is equally true that adults often find in their work a kind of joy in the act itself that relates it to play.

The essence of play is that it involves mental attitudes and is more or less spontaneous. It is a learning process of which the learner is unaware because the end for him is the activity itself. Play is not a secondary factor to be looked down upon by those who work hard; it is to be seen as one of the most expressive ways in which the human mind can work. If play has this educational value, it can also have therapeutic value. Many children who have emotional difficulties can work out their problems through play.

Children can learn about worship through the play activities of a nursery or kindergarten department in a Sunday School. One child even had "Jesus" as his imaginary companion, a fact that disturbed his parents until they saw that this was a normal function of the child's imagination in the religious context.

These flights of imagination which are part and parcel of play lead into the more transcendent elements of the meaning of religion. It takes a fertile imagination to grasp the truth of the Christmas story or the power of the Resurrection. A dull mind takes these things literally and therefore may fail to see the fundamental meaning, but a mind that has been exposed to play and stimulus of the imagination can see in these things the basic meaning of life.

As boys and girls get older, they discover the enjoyment of team play, where the members of the team are willing to dedicate themselves to the good of the group. In learning to accept the leadership of a coach or a captain, the individuals on the team are able to use their skills collectively to benefit the team as a whole. This has a great deal to do with the capacity of a child to learn to live in a covenant community, a community based upon its agreement to maintain the laws of God. What we need to do as parents and educators is to let youngsters see this parallel and to draw out of it legitimate conclusions.

When Tommy was ordered to lay down a bunt in a baseball game, he was able to advance a runner to second base, but he was out at first. He made a sacrifice in order to move a runner. The rules for the scorer are that a sacrifice does not count as a time at bat or affect the batting average. Therefore, Tommy learned that he can give up the opportunity to make a hit for the good of the team. This is perhaps the clearest example of the significance of play for understanding the place of sacrifice in life. "There is no greater love than this, that a man should lay down his life for his friends" (John 15:13, NEB).

Play is a means of renewal. As our selves develop toward maturity, we are able to see the self-expressive act in either solitary or group play as a good in itself. Play therefore brings renewal to our fading powers of personal relationship and provides refreshment for the work that we must do. It becomes the expression of our personality in the world and a form of our devotion to God.

23. *My boy has entered a period of hero-worship; how important is it that we find some good models for him?*

A growing child needs some kind of model in order to develop his sense of identity. To begin with, he can look to his parents, but as he enters adolescence, he needs other men and women with whom he can identify. This relationship differs from those he finds in his peer group, where he may or may not find an adolescent model. Teachers, pastors, casual acquaintances, men who work in the stores he frequents, movie stars and other public figures, and many others may provide the kind of model he is seeking. The important thing is to find men and women who know the difference between right and wrong, who stand firmly for their own position and yet are not so rigid as to demolish the positions of those around them. The young person needs adults who can be guides or counselors, such as he finds at summer camps or in sponsored group activities, but he also needs to find such people in his church. These are the people who are in a position to help him, because he idolizes as well as trusts them. As he develops during adolescence, he needs to see the meaning of his school work, to see the meaning of Christian vocation in relation to job opportunities, to consider the possibility of higher education, to analyze his relationships with the opposite sex as well as with his own sex, and in these ways to develop his own identity.

The difficulty in our society, with all of its complexity, is to find the kind of models that youngsters need. Adults are so confused about their own standards and purposes in today's world that this confusion is reflected in the lives of our young people. When Jimmy Dean with his angry rebellion becomes a hero figure, we are in danger of the destruction of our inherited values. When the interpretation of marriage, sex, and common honesty is taken from some of our motion pictures and television programs, we are under a great strain in finding the basic values that lead to fullness of life. This is the point at which young people's groups in the church are valuable. A well-run youth group is sponsored by two or three devoted couples in the congregation who manage, not only to be present in the youth meetings, but to be so interested in the young people that they are accepted as part of the group. This does not mean that they are just additional members of the group; they are accepted as adults in a group of teenagers. The kind of leadership they provide from behind the scenes may make all the difference in the developing insights of the members of the group. Having access to immediate models through personal relationships is much more important than idolizing some publicly acknowledged movie star or athlete. The church that can provide adult leaders who have sufficient religious faith to admit they can be wrong, who can portray in a meaningful way the heroes and saints of the Christian tradition, who are clear about Christian decisions in the modern world, and who treat the young people as persons who have their own responsibility to God, can help young people to find a meaningful position in modern life. This concern for what life means *now* makes a young people's group vital, and this can be provided only as the adults related to these young people are willing to take seriously their calling to serve God as leaders.

Only as young people come to see the significance of models whom they know, can they at the same time acquire an appreciation of the models of the past. Sooner or later they are going to begin to see the attractiveness of some of the great personalities of the Bible, particularly such men as Moses and David in the Old Testament and Peter and Paul in the New Testament. If these biblical persons are seen as truly human, with their fundamental limitations, rather than as plaster saints, the young people will be able to identify with them. Ultimately, we may hope, they will begin to see the relationship between the Jesus portrayed in the Gospels and the living Christ who stands at the center of their faith. But they are not likely to find Christ in this way unless he has been mediated to them through the loving concern of other adults in the parish. Sometimes this same sense of identity with models can be developed in a

Christian home through the activities of the family, and young people will not need the specialized attention of a young people's group in the church, but they will still need a sense of membership in the church and of being part of the worshiping congregation.

CHAPTER III

Religious Development
in the Home

*24. My husband and I want to give our boy every chance of
growing up normally. We don't want to influence his religious
beliefs. We are going to let him select his own religion. Isn't
this what most modern families are doing?*

If we look at the enrollment of the Sunday Schools throughout America, we may assume that most parents are at least ex-
posing their children to the Sunday School of a particular
denomination. How much this is influencing the children's religious beliefs is open to question, but it is perfectly obvious, if the
early years are as important as the psychologists tell us, that if
we are waiting for a child to make up his mind without
providing any positive influence, we are pointing him toward a
denial of religious beliefs from the very beginning of his life.
Sometimes parents without denominational ties may send their
child to Sunday Schools of different denominations, believing
that when he grows up he may select his own denomination
yet not be stranded without a Christian faith.

We do not usually expect one who is born a citizen of the
United States to decide, at twenty-one, whether to be an
American. Rather, we expect him to grow up as a loyal citizen
of his native country. Later on he may choose to be either a
Republican or a Democrat regardless of his parents' wishes, or
he may choose to live in any one of the fifty states, but usually
he will not change his citizenship. If he does decide to change
his citizenship, he will know, because he has been reared as

an American, what he is giving up. To bring up a child without any exposure to religion is like bringing up a child without any country whatever, so that he is not capable of making any choice about citizenship when the time comes.

If we are right in assuming that religious teaching is going on all the time in the home through what the parents are, then to let a child grow up without any religious beliefs conditions him from the very beginning of his life and makes him incapable of an intelligent choice.

25. What happens to a child when his parents try to act like God?

The Man Who Played God was the name of a successful stage play and motion picture. The plot revolved around a man who was deaf and who had learned to read lips. One scene showed him watching some lovers in a park through binoculars from his apartment window. He read their lips and discovered what their problems were, and then acted anonymously to help them.

It comes as a shock to the parents to be told they are like God to an infant. A child under three cannot grasp the idea of God, but he can accept his parents as God, and thereby satisfy his religious needs. Parents know that they can do much to make or mar a child's character, but they do not always realize that they are interpreting God to the infant through the medium of their relationship with him. In this elemental fact we find the roots of religion in the child.

Parents easily grasp the fact that they have authority over the infant. They also have the power of life and death over him, but they do not realize that this is a part of the God-relationship, or that in the feeling of absolute dependence, the child makes more of this relationship than they do. So parents are apt to accept the authority relationship on a purely secular basis and they do not keep up with the child's development.

Some parents attempt to maintain absolute authority long after the stage in the child's development that required it. By the time a child is three, he is capable of two changes in relationship with his parents. He is beginning, however vaguely, to understand that there is a power behind nature and behind his parents. He is moving out from a consciousness of his parents to God. At the same time, the authority figure of his parents is changing for him. He still may regard them as infallible until he is in school, but he expects to make some decisions on his own. The parents have changed from being a religious object to being a mediator of their own religion to the child. The parents do not always adapt themselves to these changes. There is a lag between what the children need and the parental response to these needs. In some cases this lag becomes so great that real communication between parent and child is lost. The parents maintain the authority figure that was relevant to an earlier age and the children reject it as infantile. The parents do not know that they are trying to be God to their children, but the effect is to arrest the children's religious development.

Infallible parents are effective only with children suffering from arrested development. The reaction of normal children is to rebel. The inflexible authority of parental infallibility may cause undue passivity in the children, and even when this passivity is transferred toward God, the kind of religious faith that evolves is unsatisfactory.

Even parents who try to adapt their ways to the growing needs of their children often run into antipathy toward religion during the children's adolescence. But a child whose experience of fatherhood and motherhood during infancy is unfortunate may develop a permanent resistance to religious faith. Religion begins in parent-child relationships that lead to the development of attitudes, attachments, and rejections which are expressions of the deepest forces in their personality; in this way a foundation is laid which is likely to result in sound and mature Christian faith.

The parents in a Christian family who are aware of what is happening discover that religion is taught in the home through relationships. As the parents find ways of meeting the children's needs for love and acceptance, for dependableness and law, for growth and adaptation, and for the grace of God at work in their midst, the groundwork is laid for a mature faith. Love and acceptance point to a God of love at work among us, accepting us as we are. God's self-sacrificing love is revealed in Christ's death for us while we are still sinners. Law and order point to the dependableness of a God of justice and righteousness, who has set us in a universe of natural and moral law. Growth and adaptation point to the freedom of faith, whereby we respond in obedience to God's love according to our aptitudes, as God calls us to discipleship and service. The home therefore becomes a channel of grace, in which the redemptive love of God in Christ stands behind our human love. The child responds to this with awe and reverence, at first centered in his parents and later in the almighty and holy God in whom he lives and moves and has his being.

26. What should I do about my children's prayers?

Sooner or later every child will be weaned and toilet trained, but many of us are not nearly so sure that he will learn to pray. We often show the same anxiety about prayer as we do about early training. It cannot be demonstrated that the early use of prayer by the child makes any difference in his later development. Most experts believe that as soon as the child is aware of it, he should have the opportunity to see his parents in the act of prayer, in which he may or may not join. It is much more important for him to become aware of his parents' relationship to God than it is to say some words in the form of prayer in order to satisfy his parents. If the home is one in which prayer is a normal activity, and every Christian home should be this, the child will gradually be included in the saying of grace before meals and prayer. In most homes this will include the saying of prayers before going to sleep at night; this is an opportunity for all kinds of religious and semi-religious activities.

Before the child is able to talk, it is sufficient for him to hear his mother at prayer as he goes to sleep at night. Later on he may want to learn a simple prayer. But as conversation between mother and child becomes possible, a review of the day and its activities may be more important at prayer time than formalized prayers. At the end of such a time, the mother may ask the child to thank God for a nice day or for his friends or for nursery school or for a certain teacher. If someone in the family is sick, a simple prayer expressing the child's concern may be advisable. Some parents will prefer to insert a formalized prayer such as the Lord's Prayer or special prayers suitable to children. There are many books of prayers, stories, and poetry which are quite suitable for even the youngest children. Some of these are listed at the back of the book.

27. *Are family prayers really necessary to keep the family together? How can we all participate when some of us feel awkward or self-conscious or are too young to understand?*

This question points to a fundamental difficulty in most families. I think we need to be perfectly honest here and say that in many families any kind of group family worship in the home is almost a complete impossibility except on special festivals. I am not sure that this is something to be regretted. There have been many times when a father's compulsive desire to lead his children in prayer has led to extremely negative results. I know of one young mother who had been brought up in this kind of home and who intended to take part in church work who said this: "Because my father insisted on family worship at all times and at some times to the utter inconvenience of the rest of the family, I am resolved that we will never have it in our home." This young woman had not lost her religious faith but she had seen one kind of family prayer as the hollow sham that it may be.

But there are many ways in which family prayer may be perfectly normal and natural. When the children are reasonably close in age and go to bed at the same time, they can all gather in one room with the parents and hold hands for a brief circle of prayer. It is doubtful that this will continue on into the pre-teen period, but at least it can be a start. In other cases, grace at meals offers each member of the family an opportunity in turn to say a grace that is meaningful to him. Every family will feel some desire for special prayers at Thanksgiving or Christmas or on birthdays and may wish to use these opportunities for special services of prayer. Certainly those who feel awkward or self-conscious should not be forced into positions of leadership in such situations.

Homes with musical interests may add greatly to their mutual devotions by learning to sign hymns, carols, spirituals, and other songs together. Singing graces may be used before meals. Songfests for the whole family may begin with secular songs and end with sacred ones. A collection of religious music for small children, such as *Sing for Joy,* by Norman and Margaret Mealy (Greenwich: Seabury Press, 1961), has songs marked for nursery, kindergarten, and primary school children, plus an appendix suggesting traditional hymns for use with small children. Children today listen to many recordings, and parents should encourage them to listen occasionally to good religious music, including some of the selections by the better choral groups, organ music, and the Gospel songs of Mahalia Jackson.

Children can be exposed to good art chiefly through collections of reproductions. There is a great deal of bad religious art, especially in Sunday School leaflets and sentimental religious books, and the problem facing parents is to find paintings that give a religious interpretation of reality.

Children always enjoy stories. Resourceful parents can use the story hour for all kinds of stories, secular and sacred, as well as for poetry. Bible stories may be included, but it is better to err by telling too few than too many. Any story worth telling is worth repeating many times.

It needs to be remembered that traditionally the father has been the priest in his own home. This means, for example, that when a visiting minister comes for dinner, the father still has the responsibility for leading in whatever prayer may be said at the dinner table. The ordained minister, no matter what his position, has no special standing in the worship in the home.

28. *How should a Christian family observe Christmas and Easter?*

These are the two periods of the year which are the most obviously Christian in their roots, and all kinds of possibilities open up. Some families make use of the Advent season for the lighting of special candles on the table. Others postpone certain preparations, for example decorating the Christmas tree, until just before Christmas. Sometimes they put the emphasis, not on what's going to go on in the house, but on what the family can do as a group for those who are less fortunate. Many families develop special Christmas Eve rituals, including the use of recordings, watching certain television programs, or, depending upon the custom of their denomination, going to church. Our Christmas Day in America is basically a family feast, sometimes at home and sometimes at the home of grand-parents. It is important that this family solidarity of Christmas be maintained, but not at the expense of forgetting the roots of Christmas. Practices will differ according to local customs as to when one goes to church in connection with this holiday, but certainly this should be a chief part of a family's activity in relation to Christmas.

Easter offers fewer home rituals than Christmas: Easter eggs, bunnies, and flowers. Parents should be careful to interpret these particular symbols in terms of their Easter meaning. The symbols and rituals of both Christmas and Easter have not arisen by accident but have been derived from the surrounding culture in which the church has been trying to speak; thus the Easter egg speaks of new life and the rabbit speaks of the fertility of God's world and both may be related to our faith in the resurrection of Jesus Christ.

As Easter is a church festival for all Christian people, it is helpful if the local congregation has a service to which the family may go as a unit. Where this is not possible, the parents should seek to attend with their children whatever service is open for them, even though they may later on go to a service for adults only.

A final twist is to remind parents and children alike that without Easter there would be no Christmas. Christmas by itself is the birth of the Jewish baby Jesus. Christmas seen through the eyes of Easter is the intervention of God into the life of the world and it is the Easter faith that makes Christmas meaningful. This must always be borne in mind.

29. *Our family seems to be constantly bickering. Can the Christian faith help us to stop?*

The Christian faith does not stop arguments; it keeps them from being reduced to positions of rigidity which cannot be resolved. We may distinguish between those conflicts in which there is genuine communication and therefore something significant to be gained, and the petty bickering that leads to stalemates in which one is resolved to take a position and maintain it no matter what the consequences. Any family will have conflicts unless it is dominated by one individual who forces these conflicts underground. As long as people genuinely take part in interpersonal relationships, there are going to be interchanges of opinion, conflict of wills, and in some cases outright rebellion. Only where there is ill-will or stubbornness or pride can no solution be found.

The small-time bickering that leads to constant irritation on the part of one or more members of the family is neither a genuine conflict out of which a solution can come nor a rigid position that threatens the structure of the family itself. It is usually the result of a lack of communication and an unwillingness to listen to the other side. In families where mother and father shout each other down, and so too do the children, this unfortunate situation occurs often. As nothing really serious is at stake, the primary result is a good deal of ill-will on all sides, and therefore unhappiness.

But sometimes these petty arguments can lead to broken relationships, as when we seriously offend each other, misunderstand each other, lose our tempers with the children because of fatigue, refuse to share in each other's vital interests, and reject each other. In all of these cases there is the need for reconciliation and this is the distinctive Christian factor in family life.

Insofar as the family relationships are based on a love that is willing to give of itself, there is a possibility of mending these broken relationships. Forgiveness always involves the hurt person's taking upon himself the burden of what has been done against him and then treating the offender as if this hurt had never existed. This is reconciliation; this is to be redeemed by the power of the Holy Spirit. But this is not enough; for these same conditions can occur over and over again, and although we are expected to forgive up until seventy times seven, it is much better to right the conditions that led to the original broken relationship. So we have the rediscovery of fellowship within the family which makes possible the elimination of the kind of situation in which the broken relationship has occurred. Sometimes this means a rewriting of the rules of family life, sometimes it means a rearranging of schedules, sometimes it means the recognition that either the children or the parents have certain freedoms or certain responsibilities that previously have not been clearly recognized.

The amazing thing is that where a family sees no way out of such situations, power seems to come from above or from outside through the resources of the community or through the resources of the church to make possible the mending of these relationships. This, we believe as Christians, is the grace of God at work through interpersonal relationships in the church, community, and home. This is something which is not just talked about but is experienced in the life of the Christian family.

30. *Could the church help us to order our family so that we might have time to get a deeper spiritual relationship with one another?*

This question points to the fundamental fact that, by itself, the family is not able to be an adequate intimate community. If we are to be nurtured in the Christian life, we need the help of both the home and the church. Often, however, the church succeeds in splitting up the family even in the name of increased information about family life. The church needs to do at least two things: one, to provide a ministry to the family-as-a-unit, which will be described in detail later on; and two, to give the kind of help that makes family life more meaningful on a deeper level.

This means primarily understanding what a Christian family is, what its objectives are, and what the individuals within the family should and can do to make possible the deeper spiritual relationships of a more satisfying family life. This kind of understanding develops when the channels of communication are kept open, for only as communication takes place on the current level can the channels be deepened.

There is enough talk in many families, but the concern is with inconsequential matters. There is what Gibson Winter calls "the flight from intimacy,"[1] where there is no communication in terms of the deeper meanings in life. The genuine intimacy of family life is built upon the capacity to listen and to stand together in the face of problems that may arise. But because such intimacy is difficult to achieve, most families operate in the "safe" domain of non-controversial matters and avoid crises until a blow-up occurs. They are satisfied with coexistence as a substitute for genuine companionship.

If one is willing to listen, he may very well hear the same old things on a shallow and meaningless level. But if he listens closely, he may be able to discern the deeper factors hidden in the conversation. If he listens creatively, he may draw out of the other the concerns, interests, annoyances, yearnings, and confessions that are under the surface, and the result may be either a creative interchange or an explosion. In turn, the talker may realize the importance of *his* listening also, and thus a genuine meeting may take place. If this experience is something new, the outcome may be unpredictable as both reveal themselves to each other, but a genuine intimacy on a deeper level will be reached.

This capacity to listen needs to be backed up by the acceptance of the marriage covenant: the promise to stand together. As problems, concerns, conflicts, and other topics enter into a genuine conversation, the husband and wife discover that in this deeper intimacy they need to work out their new understandings of each other. This leads to acceptance of each other as revealed in this richer relationship. Thus they are able to forgive each other and themselves, and are thereby free to communicate on an even deeper level.

Out of such communication may develop new patterns of living together, new ways of treating the children, new interpretations of authority, and new understandings of the way of God with family life. Conflicts continue and new ones will develop, but because intimacy is now at a deeper level, they can be faced and handled creatively.[2]

31. *How can I show my religion to my child? How can I help my child live a religion?*

Reuel L. Howe writes: "While we cannot equate parental action with divine action, nevertheless we can affirm that divine action takes place through human action. When such an affirmation is made and accepted as part of the parent's faith and is interpreted to the child as he is able to receive it, he is helped to grow up with a religious understanding of life itself, rather than conceiving of religion as being merely a part of life. He will grow up with the idea that being trustworthy and trusting others has not only psychological and sociological meaning, but also theological meaning."[3] This means that most of our fundamental religious teaching is not our conscious effort to tell the child anything but is the unconscious and undesigned activities of the parents whose principles propagate themselves even without their desire. The intimate bond between the parent and the child which arouses the attitude of trust is the starting point of all religious nurture. Religion begins in this parent-child relationship, for out of this relationship comes the development of those attitudes and capacities to choose which are strongly emotional but are also indicative of the work of the deepest driving forces of personality.[4]

The assumption here is that God is a living God at work in our lives. He is not an idea to be talked about so much as a personal reality to be experienced. If God is nothing but an idea, covered with logic and backed by philosophy, then we are a long way from what the Christian church means to God. We hope that the child, even before he can use the word "God," will be aware of the work of God as the creative and loving order within the home. This is something that is mediated by the parents and cannot be accomplished by anyone else. The very young child therefore does not learn to live a religion except insofar as the realities of religious faith are mediated to him through others. As time goes on, he needs to learn about God, to develop an idea of God, and to take on for himself the commitments of a mature person. But this is a long, slow process of nurture.

Basil A. Yeaxlee has summarized this process in the following way: "The parents who have mediated God through daily relationships with their children during infancy, who have taught these same boys and girls about God during childhood, and who, while admitting frankly their own imperfections and shortcomings, have lived out their own teaching as far as they are able, must when adolescence comes give their children a chance to find God for themselves and in their own way, being ready to help when help is asked of them."[5]

The biblical faith is experienced in the family when a little David finds a Jonathan in the neighborhood, when a Ruth discovers that her husband's Naomi is a wonderful person, when an Abraham and a Sarah rejoice in their first child. This faith provides the opportunity for many kinds of biblical teaching. Time after time, there are ethical decisions to be faced. Along the way, children and parents face together the problem of handling money, of stealing, of cheating, of boy-girl associations, of learning to take responsibility for one's decisions. Character is forged partly by parental example and partly by parental guidance, and in the large family the stand parents take is reinforced by the other children.

The biblical faith not only deals with the formation of character; it also interprets the meaning of life. We turn to the Bible when a parent or grandparent dies, when there is suffering and illness, when there are hard feelings or broken relations. Christ becomes not only a teacher and an example but the Redeemer, when we see that he is the turning point in history. But I do not believe that the verbalizing of this faith in Christ is of much help until it is tied in with redemptive relations in home and church, and it is this that is essential to the life of the family. If the members of the family can say of each member, "Christ died for him (or her)," the Christian faith is at work in that home.

32. Are there any special religious values in large families?

If you have six children instead of one, you have six times the blessings. Also six times the expenses. These can be measured. You buy six ice-cream cones at a time. The six quarters make a dollar and a half in the church school offering. The children grow, and the old sedan is replaced by a station wagon so that the family may have togetherness. Six pairs of hands are useful, when they are not writing on the newly painted wall in the upper hall, for they can help with the dishes, make beds, and rake leaves. Fortunately, this kind of employment can start at a relatively early age, and the wise parent can keep the hands under some kind of control through the years.

With a large family, financial outlay must be strictly impartial, especially while the children are reasonably young. I remember explaining to one of my children that if I spent five dollars on what he wanted, and still desired to be fair to the others, it would cost me thirty dollars. Since I didn't have thirty dollars, he could not have the five-dollar item. This works when they reach the stage of "It isn't fair" and can also add up to thirty.

A big family is loaded with relationships. Just think of it mathematically: Mother is related to Daddy and six others; Daddy is related to Mother and six; number 1 is related to Mother and Daddy and to numbers 2-6; number 2 is related to Mother and Daddy and to number 1 and to number 3-6. It gets very complicated when you think of the possible psychological friction. The problem is to keep the relations fluid.

It is easy for an aggressive member of the six (and most of them are that) to move into a special position, with the danger that a less aggressive child (less aggressive, not passive) may get squeezed out. If a child feels this squeeze as some kind of rejection, it may lead to a circle of rejections; and although children bounce back quickly, this may develop into a pattern. There is a certain "all-for-six-and-six-for-all" quality about a large family. As they become teenagers, the house is likely to become a teenage canteen, with the children acting as host and hostess. This means that the parents get to know other boys and girls along with their own. As long as the parents keep out of the way, except to help with the serving and with greeting people at the door, everything runs very smoothly.

It is this cohesion in a big family that is so attractive. Family meals are family gatherings, and this is true even when there are guests. When children are included at the dinner table as soon as they are old enough to sit in high chairs, they develop a strong sense of belonging to the family-as-a-unit.

Although occasionally a child gets lost in a big family, none of them suffers from "smother" love. There is simply no time for coddling. Children have ways of correcting and socializing one another. Criticisms don't have to come from the parents, for one of the older children will lay it on the line to the younger, thus strengthening the cohesion of the family. This also builds capacity for independence, so that when the children become teenagers, they can exercise more freedom in connection with responsibility.

The older children also break ground for the younger ones. The oldest one usually has to rebel more loudly and persistently than the others, but after the precedent is set, all the king's horses could not stop the younger ones from asserting the same freedom at the same age. Joint religious activities offer problems in a big family. It is not always possible for a parent to be with each child as he says his prayers. With a large age span, bedtimes and outside interests diverge so greatly that any group Bible-reading or prayer becomes difficult. But grace at the table is always possible.

There are many discussions in a large family. Most of them take place at the dinner table. They may deal with any and all aspects of the lives of the members, and often they turn to religious matters. The parents may introduce religious questions, and during special seasons (such as Lent), readings from the Bible and other religious literature may be included. Where the local church has a ministry to the family-as-a-unit, the parents can go with all of their children to Sunday School (about which there is a lengthy discussion in Chapter IV). In all of these relationships, the children and their parents are learning about religion. If you have to *tell* a child you love him, he won't believe you. Redemption is discovered when the barriers are broken down, when relations are restored, when the lost are found, when those who are dead to each other are alive again. Love is found not only in forgiveness but in the constant, sustaining power that uplifts every member of the family. When two or three (or eight) are gathered together in Christ's name, Christ is a living presence among them.

33. *One of my children wants to go to church, but the other does not want to attend. How can I help that child find a religion?*

In the last analysis, children's religious faith is not controlled by the parents. The parents can merely do the planting and the watering, for in this nurturing process, the child has the right of decision. Within God's providence, this freedom to choose is absolutely fundamental. It is to be expected, then, that in any family there will be varieties of choice among children as they enter into whatever religious maturity they are capable of.

I know of one minister's family in which one son went into the ministry, one son never goes near a church, and the third one is a nominal church member with no strong feelings one way or the other. There are some families in which all the children become active in the church and there are others in which believing parents find that all of their children turn from the church. There are so many factors in the picture that the main thing is that once we have done our job we must be willing to sit back and let the children make their own choices. It is not for the parents to berate themselves for their failure simply because the children choose to do something other than what the parents desire.

Children often do not follow the same vocation as that of their parents and in fact sometimes go against parental choices. As they grow up, they may select a denomination different from that of their parents, or none. Whatever the case, as they move into adulthood, they must be free to make their own choices.

34. *Is there anything the church can do to prepare my child for marriage? I want him to meet nice young people and to meet someone he may someday marry. When this happens, will he be prepared for marriage through education and conference with his minister?*

Most churches have a program of preparation for marriage for young people. This begins with a consideration of boy-girl relationships in the early part of high school and then moves on during the senior year of high school, either in Sunday School or in the youth group, to a consideration of the meaning of Christian marriage. Depending upon the local situation, this may or may not be a first-class and thorough covering of the subject from all possible angles. It is strongly felt in some congregations that the church is responsible for getting their youngsters ready for what is going to happen for the majority of them within the next few years, and therefore they do a reasonably comprehensive job. Most ministers today accept the responsibility for pre-marital interviews of engaged couples so that during the few weeks or months before the wedding ceremony they will be specifically prepared for marriage. This involves not only a thorough discussion of the issues of marriage but also the giving of books to the engaged couple.

It is surprising how many young people who meet in the church marry each other. It is no accident that young peoples' groups become dating agencies, for people with similar religious outlooks tend to be attracted to each other. Statistics on success in marriage indicate that similarity of religious outlook has one of the highest degrees of correlation with successful marriage. When both the bride and the groom have a similar religious outlook, this becomes the background for the beginning of their marriage and its future development.

There are many marriages in which either the groom or the bride has a different church affiliation, and therefore the minister does not meet one or the other until the very last minute. This makes adequate pre-marital counseling somewhat difficult, but most ministers are able to deal with this situation in an adequate way.

The major difficulty arises when a Protestant marries a non-Christian, a Jew, or a Roman Catholic. Then there are such differences of outlook that the marriage is not likely to have a common religious basis. Statistics show that in a great number of cases, Protestant-Catholic marriages do not work out.

35. *What is the Christian basis of family life? We would like to be a Christian family but don't know where to begin.*

"The children gather wood, the fathers kindle fire, and the

women knead dough, to make cakes for the queen of heaven; and they pour out drink offerings to other gods, to provoke me to anger" (Jer. 7:18, RSV). In this statement, the prophet Jeremiah points to the organic unity of the family, even when the religion is heathen or idolatrous. There is in this picture the organic connection of tasks, the family worship of the gods, and the one spirit unifying the family. Horace Bushnell put it this way: "I mean to assert that a power is exerted by parents over children, not only when they teach, encourage, persuade, and govern, but without any purposed control whatever. The bond is so intimate that they do it unconsciously and undesignedly—they must do it. Their character, feelings, spirit, and principles must propagate themselves, whether they will or not."[6] The family, under God, is a sacred relationship of persons even when it is a heathen family because it is part of the order of God's creation. This organic unity of the family as it is bound together by biological, social, and spiritual bonds is very important for understanding the Christian family.

Again Bushnell points out: "The impression should be made, that they themselves [parents] are struggling with infirmities; that they are humbled into a sense of these infirmities; that there is much in them for God to pardon, much for their children to overlook, or even to forgive; and that God alone can assist them to lead themselves and their families up to a better world. .... There are too many Christian families that are little popedoms."[7]

What, then, are the marks of a Christian family? The Lambeth Conference of Bishops in 1948 provided the following list. "The Christian family:

1. Seeks to live by the teaching and example of Jesus Christ

2. Joins in the worship of Almighty God on Sundays in church

3. Joins in common prayer and Bible reading and grace at meals

4. Is forgiving one to another and accepts responsibility for one another

5. Shares together in common task and recreation
6. Uses abilities, time, possessions responsibly in society
7. Is a good neighbor, hospitable to friend and stranger."

In such a family there will be the atmosphere and attitudes that reflect certain basic relationships including love, willingness to sacrifice, dependability, justice and fairness, the experience of fellowship, doing things together, having a genuine interest in each other's welfare, and a readiness to forgive each other so that broken relationships may be restored.

The place to begin is where you are. The important thing is to re-examine your family life and see how this book will help you make changes. If you do not belong to a church, it is time to seek out a church relationship. If you have done both of these things and are still unsatisfied, you need to start looking at the trouble spots in your own family life. The point is to begin where you are and to begin now, and this book is meant to help you do exactly this.

CHAPTER IV

Religion and the Schools

36. *Muriel took a Bible-story record to school, but the teacher refused to play it because "religion is against the law." Is this true everywhere?*

In certain parts of the country this is likely to happen. Because of the interpretation of the separation of church and state, some teachers feel that to introduce any kind of religious teaching into the classrooms is to go against the law. This does not necessarily reflect the teacher's opinion about religion; in fact, some teachers who are active members of churches would respond in the same way to this request. On the other hand, in other parts of the country, where readings from the Bible are required by law, there would be no question about playing such a record. We have in our country a local-option approach to the place of religion in the schools, and much depends upon the opinions of the leaders in the particular community.

As a matter of fact, if we examine the religious picture in the schools throughout the country, we find that the concept of the Protestant faith is favored. A recent sampling of our schools has shown that some practices are exceedingly common, chiefly the special activities in relation to Christmas, Thanksgiving, and Easter.[1] Bible-reading and devotional services are legally required in some states and illegal in others. Almost all schools in the far west have neither worship nor Bible-reading, whereas in the south and east a majority of schools have both. Yet, in seeming contradiction, more schools in the west have baccalaureate sermons than do schools in the east, owing perhaps to the fact that in the east there is more Catholic objection to a baccalaureate sermon by a Protestant minister. It may be concluded that the American public school is certainly not a Godless institution. Direct religious influence exists in various kinds and amounts depending upon the section of the country and the size of the community. Furthermore, it is not possible to determine the amount of religious influence that is indirectly exerted by teachers or that exists within the atmosphere of the schools themselves.

37. *My child came home from junior high school with the report that his science teacher said there was no basis for belief in God. What can I tell him?*

The problem of science and religion has been solved for most intelligent adults by seeing that religious truths cannot be scientifically tested and in fact are beyond science. For most enlightened Christians, there is no longer the contradiction between belief in God as the Creator and belief that the evolutionary process is a reasonably accurate hypothesis. It is also generally agreed that there can be no scientific demonstration of either God's existence or his non-existence. Among competent theologians, this issue seems to be closed. However, they recognize the need for a theology in this space age. Our systems of beliefs have to be recast in order to be meaningful and communicable in the modern world. Therefore, we are concerned that religious education in a space age help the child and the adult to relate himself to the world revealed by modern science.

There are not many science teachers, even in our high schools, who would say that there is no basis for belief in God. There are science teachers who do not believe in God just as there are parents and others who do not believe in God. When a child is faced with this issue on the junior high level, the important thing for the parent to do is to start at the other end with religious truth, what it means and why, and to show how, at the point where it seems to be denied by science, it is operating in the realm of personal values and the revelation of God. This kind of religious faith makes sense in a scientific world even though it cannot be scientifically validated. Even the Bible claims that no man has seen God at any time, and, according to empirical science, what you can't see you can't prove.

The kind of experience which leads us to belief in God is different from the kind one finds in a chemistry, psychology, or sociology laboratory, in that it cannot be tested scientifically.

The Christian faith, however, deals with the personal relationship between God and man. Just as I cannot give you a scientific analysis of my love for my wife, so I cannot give you a scientific analysis for my love for God. This, however, does not deny the existence either of my wife or of God. And once children begin to see that there is an area of spirit where the sense of the numinous (the holiness of God) is paramount and that this area is not reduced by the expansion of scientific knowledge, there will be little difficulty in straightening out their conflict between science and religion.

Difficulty arises when we teach the Bible in the wrong way to start with. If a child believes that the Bible's description of creation is to be taken as literal truth and then to be compared with the hypothesis of evolution, it is obvious that evolution is going to win hands down; it is simply a better literal description of what might have happened in the origin of life. But the Bible does not pretend to literal truth. It tells us that in the beginning God was the Creator and man was his creature and that man was disobedient. This is told in terms of the grand myth of creation. Call it a legend; call it a primitive story; call it poetic imagination; but don't make the mistake of accepting this as a scientific explanation of how the world began. There are many other passages in the Bible that need this same sort of treatment before we will be able to bring together our scientifically trained youngsters and the fundamental truths of religion.

38. *A black child has enrolled in Frank's first-grade class. The other children have reflected their parents' opposition. What can we do to interpret the matter positively and to help Frank develop proper racial attitudes?*

A child normally reflects the racial attitudes of his parents. If the parents have an attitude of treating all persons alike regardless of race, this is going to be expressed by the children. But if, as this question suggests, a child runs into conflict with the opinions of other children who reflect their parents' attitudes, he must receive reinforcement from his own parents. There are various ways in which this can be done. One is to talk things through in terms that a first-grader can understand. There is the possibility that when the child is told why other people disagree with him, he may accept their opinions. Then too, a child who is "color blind" as far as blacks are concerned may not change his mind when he is told that other people are making a false distinction; or he may decide that this distinction is pretty good. But these are the risks that need to be taken, and only by talking the problem through can we help the child develop the right attitude toward the black child in his class.

Sometimes the community may help him. Perhaps the church has already accepted the black child and his family into membership. Perhaps the black child and his parents have had dinner in someone's home. Perhaps there will be an opportunity to visit the black child in his home or to play with him on the schoolground. There are communities in which these activities are possible, but there are others in which a white child would be ostracized for associating too closely with a black child, and this a first-grade child would not understand. Older children, sharing their parents' attitudes, might be willing to take this risk.

39. *We have released-time classes in religion, taught by teachers representing the local Council of Churches, available for chil-*

*dren in the fourth, fifth, and sixth grades. Should I register
my child for such a class?*

Released-time classes, which are sponsored by all the Protestant denominations through a local Council of Churches in
co-operation with Catholics and Jews, provide religious education on a high level. Professional teachers are paid to do the
job and the churches underwrite the budget. The children are
released from their public school classes to go to a location
near the school where they may attend these special classes.
The content of religious instruction is based on the Bible, sometimes on the common co-operative texts of the National Council
of Churches, which supplement what is learned in the home
and the Sunday School. The assumption is that no child can
get enough religious knowledge in our present system, and
therefore extra classes are heartily recommended. There are
various kinds of systems, and some parents may wish to evaluate
the system, its curriculum, and the standards of quality required of teachers before making up their minds. A poor system
will do more harm than good. The thing to guard against is a
syllabus of the Christian faith which is unacceptable to some
parents. When this happens, it would be better not to enroll
the child.

In most cases, you can safely assume that the classes will
be good for your children. The values are in terms of increased
religious knowledge rather than increased devotion to the Christian church. But children as well as adults need all the
knowledge about religion they can get. The program as a
whole deserves to be supported, whether parents have children
of the right ages or not, because about one third of the children
enrolled in the released-time classes do not normally attend
Sunday School, and therefore this is their only opportunity to
hear the Christian message. All parents should financially support the program of released-time because it is one of the finest
missionary programs that we have in our communities to reach
children.

40. What are the values my child will receive from religion classes in a church-related day school?

There has been an increase in church-related Protestant day schools, sometimes called parochial schools, in recent years. In most cases, the demand for such schools is based on a purely secular desire for a higher level of education. This motivation is a legitimate one, for the church often has contributed to the needs of the community through hospitals and schools.

When the motivation for a church-related school is primarily religious, it may mean that religion is to be incorporated into the total curriculum, which is to be on a level higher and more effective than that of the public schools. In other words, the ideal of the school is the formation of a Christian person. This requires top-notch teachers, small classes, and extremely careful screening of the youngsters, with the perspective of the Christian evaluation of man and interpretation of the universe running through all courses. This, I suppose, would be the ideal parochial school, which could be supported by Christians of every denomination. As far as I know, few schools are on this level.

One assumption is that although the parochial school may not be any better than the public schools, its religious classes will make a tremendous difference in the character and devotion of the youngsters. There is no evidence that this is so. It has been abundantly shown by research both in this country and in England that classes in religious knowledge may increase actual information about religion under some circumstances, but that it definitely does not make any difference in terms of discernment and devotion. The increase in discernment, devotion, and character comes out of the quality of life of the Christian home supported by the believing congregation in the Christian church. Evidence for this statement is provided from various kinds of studies.

For example, there is a parochial Episcopal school in Dallas, Texas, which was evaluated against a control-group of students

of similar background and belonging to the same local congregation. With regard to real-life situations and the pupils'
attitudes to specific religious activities, there was no superiority
whatever on the part of the parochial students. The only
difference was in terms of religious knowledge.[2] In a study of
English schools, it has been shown that students actually fail
to improve their religious knowledge during their high school
years if they have no church connection, but if they are supported by their membership in an active congregation, there is an
increase in religious knowledge as well as religious devotion.[3]
The same figures apply to Catholic parochial schools in this
country.[4]

The values a child receives from a church-related school depend upon the quality of its secular program as well as its
religious training. If religion classes are taught without imagination, they may lead to such a strong emotional response that
the youngster will remain negative to religion for the rest of his
life. This is a problem that college chaplains sometimes face
with the graduates of church-related schools with compulsory
religion courses.

The point is that we have not yet solved the problem of
how to teach religion in schools in such a way that it will both
increase religious knowledge and encourage religious devotion.
The only place we see this happening is in the local congregation itself.

41. *What are the values of religiously affiliated secondary
schools and colleges?*

The answer to this question is implied in the previous one.
The first value of any religiously affiliated secondary school or
college is in terms of whether it provides a good secular
education. In this respect, some of the secondary schools of
America are absolutely top-rate. There are also religiously
affiliated colleges that maintain this high level of secular
education. Therefore, there is no particular risk of getting a

second-rate education if the religiously affiliated school or college is academically superior.

However, there are some colleges affiliated with churches which are so second-rate that their graduates cannot qualify to enter a graduate divinity school of their own denomination to study for the ministry. The emphasis on pious religious knowledge is such that the humanities and sciences are taught on too low a level. This is a problem facing both Catholic and Protestant colleges. Two questions have to be asked in order to evaluate such institutions: (1) is it a good school on purely academic and social grounds? (2) has the Christian interpretation of its total curriculum an effect on the outlook of faculty and students alike? When these two questions can be answered positively, one has a good combination.

42. What are the values of religiously affiliated summer camps and conferences?

On the whole, it may safely be said that more young people and adults gain insight into the nature of the Christian faith through these summer camps and conferences than through any other means. Here, in the fellowship of genuine Christian concern, it is possible to delve deeply into the fundamental truths of the Christian religion and to talk seriously about the application of one's faith to life.

When starting a new young people's group in a small church a number of years ago, the minister selected four young people and gave them scholarships to attend a diocesan summer conference. These youngsters came back with such enthusiasm that, as the officers of the new young people's group, they provided leadership which led, not only to fast growth in terms of numbers, but also to a program that was fundamentally sound in meeting the religious needs of the young people. This could not have happened with an average group stumbling along without such insights or with the insights imposed by some adult. Many church groups have had the same experience with adults who have returned from such conferences.

An important type of summer camp is the family church camp. In this situation families are able to live together in tents or cabins. Meals taken in common relieve the mother of the responsibility for preparing them. During the mornings, children have a program suited to their needs while the parents enjoy special classes. In the afternoons, there is the opportunity for recreation. The evenings may or may not be centered on the family, depending upon the plans for the group. Such programs often lead to a tremendous strengthening of family life.

Summer conferences and camps are available to people of varying financial status. Some churches are able to provide scholarships for the children, some conferences are set up deliberately for those who need to be in the country more than they need to hear about the Gospel, some conferences are religiously sponsored but are basically for the purpose of improving the health and physical stamina of the youngsters, and some are primarily summer refresher courses of a highly intensified kind for those adults and teen-agers who are willing to study. In all of these camps and conferences, worship may be outdoors, thus arousing a sense of the holy or the esthetic.

43. Six-year-old Susan attended a Bible-club meeting in the neighborhood and came home with the report that the lady told all the children who wanted to become Christians to go with her into another room. My daughter was disturbed and wanted to know if she was a Christian. We all belong to the church, and Susan is baptized. How should I answer her?

Here we confront the differences that exist between Christian groups. There are organizations of child evangelists who run Bible clubs that are open to all people regardless of denomination. The leaders believe that children need to be converted and are capable of making a decision for Christ at the age of six or seven. This goes against what we know about child psychology as well as about religious convictions. The result of such practices often is an antipathy toward any kind of religion or a negative reaction that may become permanent. Most parents, therefore, are careful to keep their youngsters out of such Bible clubs, however innocent they may seem to be, unless they are sure there will be no attempt at conversion of the children.

As to the answer to Susan, she should be assured that through her baptism she has become a member of the church and therefore she is a Christian; and when she is asked whether she wants to become a Christian, she should say she is one through her baptism. Here also is the opportunity for the parent to explain something of the meaning of baptism, and the next opportunity offered by the church to see a baptism should be taken advantage of. Susan can understand that a baby can be baptized, and that this is the baby's way of coming into the church and becoming a member of the family of God; and Susan can also understand that later on she will reconfirm these baptismal promises for herself. But she must wait until she is older to make such promises.

CHAPTER V

Religion, the Church, and Children

44. *An Air Force chaplain received a phone call from a mother who wanted to have her baby "done." When he asked her what church she belonged to, she replied, "Do you have to be a church member to have your baby baptized?"*

Baptism is the means whereby the child becomes a member of the church. He is incorporated into the Body of Christ by the power of the Holy Spirit. It is a means whereby God declares his relationship to the infant. The child does not make this decision. The emphasis is on incorporation and grace, not on the faith of the individual or on the blessing, although these are important in the mature decision of a Christian. The faith, which the child lacks, is provided by the parents or the sponsors who speak for the child and by the congregation that receives him. The parents, through the baptism of their children, enter an important ministry of their own. Therefore, parents should be active church members if they are to fulfill the promises they make in the name of their child.

Many churches today insist that the parents undergo some kind of training so that they may understand the implications of baptism. The parents, the sponsors, and the congregation make specific promises to undertake responsibility for the nurture of the infant, so that he may ultimately be able to ratify his baptismal vows as he is confirmed or in some other way professes his faith. The parents are helped to see that the sacrament of baptism meets the religious needs of their child. The act of forgiveness promised in baptism is a sign of God's love. The ongoing life of a congregation, with its requirements that he learn the teachings of the church and accept the demands of the Gospel, meets his need for law and order. The expectation that he will grow to maturity and make his own profession at the age of discretion indicates that he is free to grow under God's guidance. The fact that he is brought into a worshiping congregation helps him to develop his awareness of the mysterious holiness of God, leading finally to the full community of participation in the Lord's Supper.

But baptism cannot have these meanings without the ministry of the parents. This is why the practice of pre-parental counseling and education has arisen, especially for parents who are expecting their first child. The parents learn that these early days of a child's life have much to do with his later acceptance of the Christian faith. Many churches also provide classes to assist parents in understanding their parental roles. Horace Bushnell wrote that "the child is too young to choose the rite for himself, but the parent, having him as it were in his own life, is allowed the competence that his own faith and character will be reproduced in the child, and grow up in his growth, and thus the propriety of the rite as a shield of faith will not be violated."[1]

45. We do not believe in infant baptism. What does the church offer to those who want to wait until their child is ready for believers' baptism?

Many parents, especially members of the Baptist and Christian churches, believe that baptism should be by immersion at the age of discretion, which is called "believers' baptism." As there is no evidence in the New Testament of the baptism of babies, there is no reason for infant baptism today. A child should make his own act of faith.

But what happens to the child during these early years? Some would say that he comes under the care of the church through the faith of his parents. Therefore, parents have a responsibility similar to those who have their infants baptized. They have the responsibility to love and guide their children, to provide for their nurture, and to open to the children the channels of God's grace. But many churches offer no rite or sacrament, and some offer no guidance to parents.

Some churches now provide an act of dedication. This may be a dedication of the child or a dedication of the parents. It is a public recognition of the responsibility of the parents and the congregation for the nurture of the child, with the expectation that such guidance will lead to baptism and membership in the church at the age of discretion.

Psychologically, the effect is much the same as that of infant baptism as far as the sense of dedication is concerned. Theologically, there is a difference; and this is the point at which parents must make their own decision.

46. *Why does baptism involve a promise, a responsibility that is too difficult to keep? We did not have our children baptized after we learned that it meant being active in the congregation.*

Parents who are not interested in the church and who think of baptism primarily as a social function have difficulty in taking on the promises involved in baptism. If they cannot seriously make these promises on the part of the child, they are quite right in refusing to have the child baptized. Too often in the past, baptism has been so easy that it has been reduced to merely a social function. It is done because it will make grandmother happy or because it is the respectable thing to do or because it is the occasion for some kind of party.

Baptism normally takes place within the framework of the church's worship—ideally, either in a special service for families or at the regular service on Sunday morning. It involves not only the commitment of the family but also the acceptance of responsibility on the part of the congregation, and therefore should not take place outside the community of faithful people. Just what active responsibility should the parents assume in the congregation is open to question. Some ministers would go so far as to say that the parents must make a pledge to the church, agree to attend church regularly, and promise to bring their children every Sunday to the nursery or to whatever activity is available for infants. Other ministers would not be so rigid about this, but almost all of them today insist at least on more than nominal church membership.

47. *I think it is nice that my child attends Sunday School. However, his teacher never calls on me. Is there anything I should do to help what he is doing, or does the church take care of everything?*

There are all kinds of Sunday Schools. Some are good, some bad, some indifferent. A good Sunday School is one of the most effective instruments we have for the formation of Christians. It reflects the quality of life of a congregation and is based almost entirely on the conviction, understanding, competence, and contagious faith of the teaching staff. A competent teacher seeks to understand the children, and one of the best ways to do this is to call at the children's homes and see what their family background is.

One teacher, after calling at the homes of all of her children, came to the conclusion that half her class was in need of a mother substitute, because they lacked the kind of mother love that was essential to good Christian training. The other five in the class came from homes in which the parents were active church people and came to the family service with their children. They needed an entirely different kind of treatment. This teacher was particularly sensitive to the needs of all ten of her children and therefore was able to treat each one in terms of his particular family background. This would have been impossible if she had not visited their homes. Sometimes through these home calls the teacher is able to enlist the assistance of a parent who otherwise would have no understanding of the purpose of the Sunday School.

Certainly the church cannot do it all. Almost all research

in this area indicates that it is the co-operation of home and church that is crucial for religious development and character formation, and therefore the parents should be involved in their children's religious nurture.

48. *Too often I feel that children are sent to Sunday School simply because it is the thing to do. Why should we send our children?*

It is interesting to examine the reasons why parents send their children to Sunday School. Often they are motivated by the desire for respectability, or a particular kind of social standing, or the opportunity to dress up on holidays, especially on Easter, or some other purely secular reason.

These parents have very low expectations as to the results. They expect that Sunday School will help their children fit into the status behavior associated with the church in a secular society.

Sunday School may lead to the realization of such goals, and to some degree they may be desirable, but they are obviously side effects. There is one chief reason for sending a child to Sunday School: so that he may come to know Jesus Christ as Lord and Savior and accept him in his own life. This means to become an active member of the Body of Christ. The child learns, "My bounden duty is to follow Christ, to worship God every Sunday in his church; and to work and pray and give to the spread of his kingdom." If he takes this seriously, it is more than many parents have bargained for.

49. *Should I make my child go to Sunday School?*

There is no easy answer to this question, for any solution depends on a number of factors: "Is the program worth while?" "Do you attend with him?" "What alternatives are there?" "How old is the child?"

In some cases the program of Christian education may be of doubtful quality, so that the child is not interested or is being educated in the wrong way. Parents need to find out what is happening in the church school before they have the right to compel a child to attend. This investigation should take into account the atmosphere in which the program is conducted, in terms of worship and fellowship, of order and discipline. The parents should also become acquainted with lesson materials and teaching methods, and should know the aims and objectives of the entire church program.

If this investigation indicates that what is occurring leads to genuine Christian education, almost all children should be compelled to attend regularly. Christian education is more significant than secular education, and although we do not often hear of parents who refuse to let their children attend school, there are those who don't consider a Christian education as necessary.

But should you ever *send* a child to church school? Many experts are not convinced that one hour on Sunday, without parental support and co-operation, has any cumulative educational value. Research indicates that when parents *bring* their children to a family-centered church, the results are more favorable. A program of worship with the family in church together, followed or preceded by separate classes for children and parents, provides a shared experience which becomes the basis for religious growth during the week.

A movement in this direction is based on the recognition that the family's organic unity is God's purpose, and that this unity leads to an enduring Christian nurture. The question then becomes, "Shall the family attend church school together?"

This does not eliminate rebellion, but it places the spirit of an organically united family squarely behind church school attendance and the development of Christian nurture in the home.

The problem arises with differing degrees of intensity at various ages. If a child under twelve rebels, the chances are that the program of the church is unsuited to the child. Otherwise a mild amount of pressure will result in willing obedience, especially if the family attends together. Parents who become involved at this point may do much to improve the quality of life in the church. By attending with their children, demanding better lesson materials, studying the situation and making suggestions, they may add to a high level of efficiency within the enterprise.

With teenagers, the problem takes on many new complications. The teenager is under a new set of pressures, especially from those of his own age group. If his friends either do not attend any church school or are Catholics or attend a different church, he may rebel because there is no motivation for continued attendance. Even if his parents and other children attend, he may rebel to express his independence. This is likely to happen especially when the parents take their faith seriously, but then the rebellion is meaningful. Children of ministers or of pillars of the church are more likely to rebel at this time than are children of nominal church members.

There are no simple rules to guide parents at this point, especially if there are a number of children in the family. If the oldest child refuses to attend and is successful in maintaining this stand, each of the others will take the same stand as soon as he dares. But even if the oldest has not rebelled, the others may. Each case must be handled individually.

Some teenagers will tell you that they no longer believe in Christianity. They are still looking for tasks equal to their strength, while the church talks about their needing strength equal to their tasks. Others find that their advanced courses are repeating the same biblical material they had in the fifth grade, and they are frankly bored with it. What they do not realize is that in their struggle for independence and maturity, they need what Christianity has to offer: a dominant sentiment or a center of loyalty or an integrating factor that is offered by Christian faith. There are teenagers who have discovered this and have become converted, and they want to become full members of the church. They are impatient with the church school and instead attend church, and if the church makes a real place for them, they continue to worship with the adults.

The problem cannot be solved in a parent-child relationship in isolation. The quality of church life, the nature of the neighborhood, the variety of schools, and the pressures of the gang are involved. Parents can do much to solve the problem if they take a long-run view.

If rebellion is serious, the question of alternatives arises. If it is assumed that some kind of Christian education is desirable, the child may choose another Sunday School in preference to the one he's been attending, and among teenagers, the yearning to be with the gang is sufficient motivation to attend another church.

Another alternative is to say, "You don't have to go to church school unless you want to, but it is understood that if you do not go, we will spend the same time in the study of religion at home. Watching TV or reading the funnies is not an alternative." If such a schedule is maintained, it is likely that the child will elect to return to church school and be with those his own age in preference to a tutorial plan at home. Some parents have successfully maintained such a home system when no satisfactory church school is available.

Good church schools have much less difficulty with dropouts at all ages than do poor ones. A church school with good morale, consistent leadership training, adequate time for class sessions, and genuine concerns for the needs and welfare of the children has high attendance records for all ages. Even adolescent rebellion is reduced when the program is based on the real needs of the teenagers and they are made to feel wanted and important in the life of the church. Concerned parents can do much to bring about the realization of these goals.

It is harder to buck other pressures. In a neighborhood that is not predominantly Protestant, children going to church school will see their school mates at play. A downtown church that draws from ten different public schools has no natural nucleus of friends in class. When the gang decides that church-going is unacceptable, the pressure is heavy upon each individual.

Family solidarity helps to overcome these difficulties until the time when the teenager prefers the company of others than his family; after this, there is little the family can do. However, if the whole family selects a nearby church where school mates often go, the complaint "I want to be with my friends" need not arise.

Some parents try giving their teenagers a leave of absence. At a certain point, rebellion becomes so consistent and unpleasant, and damaging to the welfare of the rest of the family who want to attend, that the parents think it wisest to give in, hoping that the freedom to choose will result in a return to church or the selection of another one. No parent can predict how risky this may be. Within a month or a year, the teenager may return to church, join a choir or young people's group, or attend on special occasions. Or he may rejoice in continuing to resist the appeal of the church on what seems to be a permanent basis.

Most of what we have said applies to teenagers. The reason is clear: most rebellion comes at this point. We can keep the child in Sunday School (if it is a good one) without too much pressure for the first twelve years. In many cases, praise be, no rebellion occurs and our high school classes continue to be surprisingly large. But when the teenager rebels, we have to play it by ear.

I think there is a long-range program which can be recommended. Start attending Sunday School with your child as soon as possible. Make this family attendance a weekly affair, including both parents. Maintain this regularity through the years so that even if a teenager rebels, he will have had the experience of the organic unity of a Christian family in the church. Then he may not rebel, or if he does, he will probably be drawn back to the church in a short time.

We need to remember that all we can insist upon is attendance: no one can compel another to have faith in the God of Jesus Christ—not even God himself. Faith comes by grace, and God gives us the freedom to resist his love. We must give our children the same kind of freedom, in the hope that they will respond in faith to God's grace.

50. *What should teachers be teaching my child in Sunday School? What do I look for in a good Sunday School for my child?*

Ideally the purpose of Christian education is to share in the redemptive life of the fellowship of the Holy Spirit *now*. The teacher becomes a channel of God's grace, through whom God acts to restore the learner to the right relationship with him. The content of the Gospel, the development of Christian character, and membership in the church provide the structure of this relationship. But no content, no method, no moral law, and no meeting of requirements of membership can be a substitute for the Gospel itself. When one faces up to this demand, that through one's teaching the child is going to know that Christ died for him, that through the experiences of the classroom a pupil is going to find balm for his soul, that through being a member of the congregation a learner is going to become a new creature, it is enough to scare the clergyman, the teacher, and the parent.

Now, no one wants to admit that he fears the demands of the Gospel. He prefers to find objection in other areas. Parents and teachers alike complain: "It takes too much time"; "It demands trained teachers"; "It puts pressure on the minister"; "It uses modernistic or progressive teaching methods"; "It doesn't use enough Bible"; "It makes the parents go to church school." These objections are made sincerely and are to be taken seriously because these complaints point to the real demand that is placed upon us.

Let us look at this demand from a biblical point of view. The Bible tells a story of God's acts in history. It tells us that God created all that is and saw that it was good. It tells us that man rebelled and was cast out of God's presence. But God sought an agreement with Abraham, and this covenant was for man's redemption. This covenant turned on the law, and Israel failed to keep the law. This led to futility, but also to the hope of a Messiah. The turning point in the drama came when God took upon himself the consequences of man's sin, and through Jesus Christ reconciled the world unto himself. No longer did salvation depend on keeping the law, for now a man was justified by faith. This was followed by the gift of the Holy Spirit and the formation of the church.

This is the point at which everyone enters the biblical story. Through our baptism we are made members of the Body of which Christ is the head. As members of the fellowship of the Holy Spirit, we grow in grace and seek to fulfill our vocations as servants of God. We have inherited the history of the Old and New Covenants; the history of the Jews and Christians is our history. We, too, have been created; we, too, have known the law which convicts us of sin; we, too, are those for whom Christ died. So we come upon the stage of history in which we are members of Christ, and at this point we also stand under God's judgment. We face this judgment without fear and with hope because we know ourselves as redeemed sinners and not as sinless saints.[2]

When the Bible is seen theologically, placing a demand upon us to identify ourselves with the biblical story, it is relevant at every stage of our development. Even a little child has been created, has known the law, has been loved as he is, and has been baptized, and faces death and judgment. When the Bible is taught in this way, trained teachers are required. It takes time to discover how to communicate the saving truth of God to children who cannot talk in the language of the Bible. Ministers become the chief pastors of children and adults together in the community of the Holy Spirit. Families worship together in the congregation of Jesus Christ.

Furthermore, if we are to understand the theological demand of the Gospel, we find that it meets normal human needs. Everyone needs to be loved and accepted as he is, but as one teacher said of an ornery child: "Christ may have died for him, but why should I?" But this is exactly the point. We must let the children come to us as Jesus did. Only by grace are we enabled to do this, and thus there is a theological demand that we fear because we cannot achieve it except by the power of God. Only as the Sunday School class becomes a group in which all are accepted as they are, can Christian teaching occur. Within such an atmosphere, discipline provides structure and therefore is not resisted. In addition, there is freedom to grow in grace on the part of the entire group. In these personal relationships, God is at work healing our relationships and sustaining our love.

Where this atmosphere is achieved, Christian nurture is occurring. But often such an atmosphere becomes impossible because of the refusal of members of a congregation to admit they are redeemed sinners. Because they believe they are sinless saints, they do not feel compelled to accept others as they are. The quality of life of a congregation is the primary demand that has to be met before Christian education can take place, and those who believe they are without sin are like the elder son who cannot accept the prodigal.

The escape from this demand of the Gospel is disguised in many ways. One of these is so-called Bible-teaching, by which we find the attempt to master the content of the Bible without seeing its relevance to life or to our place in the ongoing drama by which God redeems mankind. Just as the devil can quote Scripture for his purpose, so we can learn the Bible for the wrong reasons.

Another escape is in moral teaching. "Sunday School stuff" is a term of reproach because it refers to an unrealistic set of moral standards that are not applicable to life. Paul made it clear in the Epistle to the Romans that he knew what was right, but that he did what was wrong, and he had no power to change this because "sin" had possession of him. We do not change people morally by telling them. God changes people because they are moved by grace to have faith.

These requirements of a good Sunday School, which seem to

demand so much educationally, are actually based on the Christian faith. If our beliefs are correct, then the message must be derived from their Christian purpose. If the quality of life of a congregation is essential to Christian teaching, then it is proper to demand that at least a central core of a congregation have an insight into the redemptive and sustaining power of the Gospel. If the teachers must become channels of grace, then it is proper to insist on adequate teacher-training of those who care enough to submit to such discipline. If the family is seen in its Jewish-Christian framework, with the ministry of the parents as essential, then parents' classes are mandatory. If the means of grace come to the congregation in its common worship, then it is proper for families to worship together in a service geared to the family-as-a-unit. If it takes time for a group to operate in a fellowship, the requirement for fifty-minute classes is normal. If the male and female influence provides a Christian family atmosphere in the classroom, there might well be two teachers for every class. These are all theological reasons for the demands of a good church school and not the gadgets of progressive educators. It is true that we have learned from modern methodology and from group dynamics, but the New Testament has already told us that when a teacher retires to the wilderness with twelve pupils, this is the best method. Life-centered questions are not only those asked today but those asked by Jesus and of Jesus. The discussion method is not new. And when stories are used as a basis for preaching in the family service, one does not have to look far into the Gospels to find this method used by the Master.

No Sunday School is going to meet all of these requirements, but where intelligent parents are enlisted in the life of the church, it is possible for the local congregation to move in these directions. This is the kind of thinking going on in the seminaries today, and many of our ministers know that this is an accurate statement of the goals of Christian education in the church.

51. How can the religious training of the church help my child develop a sense of direction in his life? Will this training help him to accept authority and keep him from being a delinquent?

The focal point of Christian training is Jesus Christ. This centering of our faith on Jesus Christ may or may not be effective in providing direction in life. In some Sunday Schools, Jesus is seen simply as a man in a long robe and with a beard, who lived a long time ago and who loved children. This happens to be true, and at a certain age this is as much as some children can understand, but it hardly acts as a motivating force in one's life. If you ask a teenager who provides direction for his life, he may very well point to certain adults, including his parents, some of his teachers, leaders of youth groups, and others from contemporary life. Rarely, even in church groups, will Jesus Christ be mentioned. To all intents and purposes, Jesus was dead and buried two thousand years ago and is irrelevant as far as life today is concerned.

This, it seems to me, is a fault in our contemporary teaching. We have not helped children to identify with any of the great characters from the history of the church in such a way that they share in the struggles, temptations, and sustaining power that God had offered to these people. Without this sense of the dynamics of decision, a person today will not choose a model from the past. The weakness of much Christian education is that when heroes are presented as models, they appear as plaster saints who had no real problems to overcome. It is even assumed, in the case of Jesus, that the temptations he faced were not real temptations and that he really could not have given in to Satan. This unreality in our approach to the heroes of the past has left them helpless in influencing the present. The problem here is to recapture the reality of their temptations and their decisions and their genuine heroism in terms that are relevant to the current period.

When a congregation shares a living sense of God and his claim on us, there is a very good chance that the child will develop a sense of direction in his life. He will be stimulated to try to find the basic meaning in the events of his life, to root out and identify the religious issues of his day-to-day living in family, school, and community, and to interpret his discoveries in terms of his hopes and fears for the future. This dynamic kind of instruction helps a child become integrated as regards the person of God and his own values.

There is no guarantee that going to church will automatically make a child either accept authority or avoid delinquent behavior. The point is that a church that provides the right kind of support and belief for a child will help him see where authority really lies, enable him to discover the relationship between his freedom and responsibility in society, and provide the kind of emotional and psychological support that will make delinquency a less tempting form of behavior. The child who knows where he stands, who is secure in his sense of love of God and of his parents and of the members of the congregation, is not likely to need delinquent action to assert his importance. This inner direction inculcated by religious faith makes it possible for a man to stand up against the pressures of the world around him, whether they be those of a delinquent gang or of a dishonest corporation. A high sense of integrity often emerges in those who see the relevance of religion to life.

52. How can the church help my child find out who he is?

The basic problem of finding the answer to the question "Who am I?" is related to the twin question "Who are you?" Both are asked implicitly by a baby long before he can verbalize them, and he discovers the answers by the way he is treated by his parents. The parents also, if they are continuing to grow, discover anew who they are in relation to their child. The earliest years of a child's life are the most crucial in answering these fundamental questions. It goes back to the period of feeding and care, to the mother's giving of tenderness or neglecting the child, to the mother's sharing of joy or irritability, to her anxiety which is something which rubs off on the child, and to the other relationships of the household including the father and the other children. As the child grows older, his discoveries are substantiated in school and church, but he already has the fundamental inheritance of these early reaction patterns, which will stand him in good stead as he faces the more difficult and complex patterns of life as he grows up.

Religious training contributes to the answer to the question first of all in terms of the parents' own religious faith. This faith is caught by the child in terms of the relationships established by the parents in these early days. The church's contribution here is indirect, but, if what we have said about baptism and early training is carried out, the child is being prepared for the Christian answer as to who he is by the ministry of his parents.

When the child first enters the life of the church in prenursery and nursery class, he learns more about who he is by the way he is treated by his teacher and the other children. Their evaluation of him may cause him to revise the image of himself he has gained through his experiences at home, but the influence of the home is still uppermost at this time. If what happens in church is unpleasantly contrary to what he is experiencing in the home, he may react against the church even in this early period, just as later on he may react against school. Therefore, in finding out who he is, he needs resources to face others who will treat him differently. There must be some continuity between the way he is treated in the home and the way he is treated in church and school. Otherwise he will become confused about the answer to these questions.

As he grows older, he will be able to vocalize his questions and to seek words to explain his answers. At this point, the Gospel is helpful in establishing his own worth. Jesus' teaching about the significance of children and their value in God's sight has much to do with his fundamental freedom from anxiety and sense of security in God's world. It is important for a child to know that Jesus said, "Let the children come to me and forbid them not." Similarly, he should know that, according to Jesus, if anyone harmed a child, that person should have a millstone put around his neck and be cast into the sea. In learning from the church that Jesus Christ was willing to die for all men, which means also for each man, the child discovers that his life is so valuable in God's sight that God permitted the Son of God to be crucified for his sake. He learns too, that man is so precious in God's sight that the very hairs of his head are numbered. And, finally, he discovers that "God made man for immortality." "In Christ God was reconciling the world to himself," and the promise is that those who believe in Christ should have eternal life.

These words may be merely empty phrases if the church members act in such a way as to deny the truth of this evaluation of man. The little child who sings "Jesus loves me, this I know," may discover that the church refuses to tell him so. Unless God's love is mediated in the Christian family and in the Christian church, there is very little chance that the child will come to know who he is.

53. *We plan to bring up our children as Christians, but why do they have to go to church regularly?*

It is possible to bring up children according to certain value patterns without going to church. But our insight into the nature of Christianity points to the need for membership in the church. The Christian religion arises as a result of the relationship between God and his people. The emphasis is upon the church as the Body of Christ, which means that the members are connected with the Body in the same way that one's fingers or eyes or ears are related to the human body. This organic relationship between the individual and the corporate nature of the church is distinctive of the Jewish-Christian tradition. The Bible speaks of the church as the bride of Christ, as the people of God, as the household of faith, as the community of the Holy Spirit, or as followers of the way.

In these and other ways the New Testament indicates that we who are Christians belong together, primarily in our worship of Almighty God.[3]

This emphasis on the organic nature of our unity makes the worshiping congregation the most significant element in the ongoing life of the church. One simply cannot be a Christian in isolation. To be a Christian means to belong to the Body, to be grafted onto the vine.

This does not mean that we should spend all of our life within the church building. As Christians, we are the church in the world, and our task is to do the work of the church in the world rather than "church work" in the church. A Christian, as part of a worshiping congregation, finds that the claim of God upon him is to act as a Christian in the world. This involves making decisions in economic and political movements as well as in personal and home life. The Christian faith demands an ethic which is both personal and social. The realization that the questions of individual ethics and of the human rights of all men in all fields of co-operation can never be answered in isolation from each other, but only in terms of a total claim of God upon us, involves us in the life of the church.

The starting point of all Christian nurture can be seen: The pupil comes from the world to the church and then returns to the world. He lives in a society in which rapid social change is taking place, and in that society he must live meaningfully as Christ's soldier and servant. If he finds in the church what ideally should be there, he gains perspective by which he can evaluate the experiences he brings to the church and he finds out what it means to be a Christian in the world.

54. How can I help Tom decide his own religion for himself? At what age is he able to decide? When should he join a group?

Psychologically a child is capable of making a decision for

himself at about the age of fourteen. In some churches this age is moved a little lower, say, to twelve, and in others it is boosted to sixteen or eighteen. One competent minister believes that if he can have his ninth-graders for one full year of specialized training, they will make an intelligent decision at the end of that year. What is involved is the emerging of a dominant sentiment or the centralizing of motivation. As Tom enters adolescence and seeks to stand on his own feet, he becomes capable of making more and more decisions on his own responsibility. At this time he can decide whether to be confirmed or to make a profession of faith or to follow whatever the practice of the local congregation is.

In some churches, because of traditional practices, it is expected that an adolescent will make his decision at a particular time. This leads to a mild form of coercion or manipulation in which the young person does not feel free to refuse, and rather than make a scene he proceeds to go through the motions of making his decision. This is particularly true in cultures where social pressures surround confirmation.

Responsible parents will see to it that Tom has an opportunity to make a decision during this period, but it should be clear to Tom that he is free to say "yes" or "no" and that he will not be coerced or manipulated by his parents, the minister, or the group. During the period prior to confirmation, he should have an opportunity to be in a young people's group in the church. These groups usually operate for those of junior high school age and over, and are effective in building loyalty to the church when they are properly directed. After the time of decision, the group of young people in the church continues to be the focus of the young person's activity, as it should be, and this may be exceedingly valuable in helping him in his religious growth. During this same period, from junior high through high school, summer camps and conferences are most valuable in helping to bring about really intelligent commitment to Jesus Christ and his church.

55. I feel the need for new inspiration, but church worship and the sermon don't give this to me. Why can't the church offer some big men to preach and teach?

Many services of worship including the sermon are not the most inspiring that we could hope for. On the other hand, when we begin to look at the purpose of worship and of preaching, we begin to see that the responsibility for listening is just as important as the education and training of men for the ministry. Let us look at a preacher and see what is involved.

The task of the preacher is to proclaim the Gospel. There is nothing else for him to preach except the good news that God in Christ was reconciling the world to himself. This is not simply a story of what happened almost two thousand years ago; it is a retelling of the story of God's mighty acts in the light of it's relevance to today. There is no area of life from which Jesus Christ can be outlawed.

The Gospel speaks to your life in the congregation, to your life in a Christian family, to your relations with all men. It is as concerned with school problems, race problems, good housing, and politics as it is with personal relations.

"Preaching," said Phillips Brooks, "is a communication of truth by man to men." Even the poorest preacher may succeed at this point. The worst sermon I ever heard led me into the ministry. When you hear a sermon, you need to ask yourself just one question: "What is *God* trying to say to *me* through the words of the preacher?" And God will say different things to each person. For one it will be the call to repentance; for another it will be balm for a troubled soul; for another it will be an invitation to enter some battle for social righteousness; for another it will be an insight into a new way of behavior.

God uses the preacher as an instrument. Some instruments have greater volume or finer tone, but all may be channels of God's music. A crystal set can bring the message just as well as a hi-fi set. The preacher who calls attention to his own wisdom and to himself is a failure as a preacher because the instrument has got in the way of the music.

As a preacher, he is the watchman or sentinel. He is called to give warnings. If a congregation does not heed the sound of the trumpet, their doom is their own fault. If they listen, they may become aware of God's claim on them.

There is no doubt that much preaching must be unpleasant to the congregation, for the preacher is a prophet who can read the signs of the times, and a congregation ignores his warnings at their own risk. When the congregation is a community of reconciliation, a fellowship of the Holy Spirit, in which Christ's redemptive love is at work, the preacher has complete freedom of the pulpit.

But the minister is more than a preacher or prophet. His ministry of reconciliation is channeled through the sacraments of baptism and the Lord's Supper. The minister is the instrument for Christ, and God in Christ gives us the power that comes from the sacrament. The refreshment of our souls is God's gift, but we in the church believe that the means whereby this sacrament is given is the ministry.

The church has been described as a congregation of faithful people, in which the Word of God is preached and the sacraments are duly administered. The redemptive love of God sustains a member of a congregation because of his faith. What he receives through going to church is God's bounty in response to what he has brought to him in the church.

In modern language, such a congregation learns to accept the fact that God accepts each individual as he is, and therefore each member is given power to accept those whom he would otherwise reject. Out of this basic ministry comes the program of the congregation with its pastoral care, its Christian education, its organization and administration—all of which exist for only one reason: to open the channels of God's love in our midst.

The problem in many churches is to find this kind of fellowship, this kind of mediation of God's love. And this is not always easy. If we can't find it anywhere, we had better look pretty closely at ourselves.

56. Our minister helps families in time of trouble, and we need the church at those times, but why do we have to attend social groups at church regularly? I enjoy other charities more.

Many churches are over-organized, and there are so many meetings going on that there is no chance for genuine Christian fellowship. Too many meetings tear the family apart, sometimes make for busywork in the name of Christ, and often take away from the opportunity for genuine study of what the Christian faith is all about.

The real justification for groups in the church is the deepening of the roots of our religious faith and the increasing of our insight into what we can do as Christians in our own particular area of competence. They may also be valuable in providing the simple fellowship that Christians need to share with each other. Christians, however, are doing their work as Christians when they assume their responsibility in the various social agencies and other worth-while organizations in the community. In fact these organizations probably would not function nearly as well if they were not backed by Catholics, Protestants, and Jews who see their citizenship being expressed in these secular ways.

I think that each individual has to pick and choose in order to find the niche in which he can operate most effectively in terms of his sense of Christian responsibility. Some people find that the church offers more opportunities, whereas others prefer secular groups. This is a matter for individual choice.

The implication in the first part of the question, however, is that since the church and its ministry may be valuable as trouble-shooters for families, we ought to be able to call on the church in times of emergency even though we are not carrying our load in the church at other times. If the church is going to minister to us in times of crises, of sickness, of death, perhaps we had better be sure of our interpersonal relationships in the congregation, so that channels will be open whereby the healing power of God may come to us. A minister or fellow Christian who is a complete stranger may seek to help us with all the good will in the world, but he will be hindered by his lack of acquaintance with our needs and our hopes. Furthermore, if we are only on the receiving end, and have never given of our Christian love to others in equally dire circumstances, we may not be able to receive graciously. The road must be kept open in both directions if we are to give and receive help.

CHAPTER VI

Religion, the Church, and Youth

57. I want Sally to be confirmed. After all, that's what we have been sending her to Sunday School for. She said she doesn't believe all that "Jesus stuff." I could hardly believe my ears, and somehow I can't convince her that she should believe the Bible and the church. Can you help me?

This question indicates that the reason for going to Sunday School is to be confirmed or to accept believers' baptism or to make a profession of faith. The great tragedy of American church life is that many young people accept this interpretation and use this act as a means of graduation from all relationship with the church. The interesting point is that Sally has reacted against this Sunday School type of teaching before she has faced the decision to be confirmed, and has, in her freedom, expressed her right to responsible doubt. The mother, in the face of this, is trying to convince Sally to believe the Bible and the church in spite of her own inclinations.

If this were brought to me as a pastoral situation, I would tell the mother to thank God that Sally has enough integrity not to go through with a pious act that would be a fraud. Here is a girl who has had enough sense to question what she has been handed and therefore needs the kind of help the church can offer in thinking these things through. This right to doubt is not the peculiar property of the adolescent but belongs to all of us who are Christians, for unless we can give a reason for our belief, we may be sure that the faith cannot stand up in the world of modern science and technology.

What Sally needs is not pressure on her to be confirmed but a chance to talk through all of her doubts and to be provided with those resources whereby she may seek for answers that will be adequate for her.

58. A fundamentalist Youth for Christ group has become active in our suburban community, and our youngsters are quite excited and enthused about their meetings. They now want to stop attending our church youth group because they feel it is not exciting enough and does not deal with issues they are concerned with. What can we do as parents to help the church develop an adequate youth program?

The answer to this question should have been anticipated several years previously. Most likely the local church group does not have the right kind of parental advisers, and has become a sitting duck for the militant fundamentalist point of view of a competing youth group.

Youth groups in the church need to have a large place for self-government and a program based on study, worship, service, and recreation. An effective youth group combines a great amount of self-government with the most careful and yet subtle supervision. The adult leaders are resource persons, fully trusted by the young people and yet working primarily in the background. Young people need assistance when they ask for it, and at the same time they resent any imposed planning by adults. Programs pleasing to the young people do not just happen; they are the result of careful consideration of interests, goals, and procedures. The advisers, usually including one or more couples from the parents in the congregation, and the executive committee need to plan the meeting carefully. The advisers may feed into the hopper certain suggestions of activities and programs, but by the time these ideas reach the members of the group, they should have been incorporated by the executive committee and presented by them. The youth groups in the local congregation may reach out in various directions in order to tie in with other youth groups and to participate in denominational and interdenominational activities. Sometimes they promote church summer camps and conferences.

The danger is that the youth group will become a separate organization with no organic connection to the life of the total congregation. The young people need to feel that they are full-fledged members of the redemptive community in the local parish and then they will be free to be themselves within the structure of specific groups and activities that are theirs.[1]

59. Will participation in the youth fellowship of the church guard Barbara against promiscuous dating and unhealthy habits?

There is no guarantee that membership in a youth group in the church will change Barbara's basic motivations and urges. Whatever previous character development has occurred will have its opportunity of expression in and through a youth group. Some youth groups have few controls and poor programs and are primarily for the purpose of socializing and unsupervised dating. The parents may assume that a church meeting will be carefully controlled, but they should make sure this is so. Even when the youth group is well supervised, there is no guarantee that this will affect what happens afterward; and some parents are careless about letting their youngsters do as they please after the meeting is over. Such activities may be perfectly innocent but, again, this depends on whether or not the parents can trust the youth and not on the conditions under which they are operating.

A well-run youth program, in which the planning has been worked out by the young people themselves with the intelligent advice of trusted adults, is based upon worship, study, service, and recreation. The activities are geared to the interests of the young people and are pointed in the direction of the religious issues in their own lives. This means that they will be dealing with topics that are dynamic and important to them,

that the worship will be relevant to their lives, that the opportunities for doing things for others will be realistic and worth
while, and that the recreation will be healthy and invigorating.
With the aid of such a program, we may expect Barbara to
be helped in making intelligent Christian decisions about her
activities, so that she will see more deeply into the meaning of
life and so that her relationships with others will be on a healthy
basis. Parents may expect this kind of direction when the youth
fellowship is a reflection of the quality of life of the congregation
as a whole.

Marjorie Reeves, in a remarkable little book called *Growing
Up in a Modern Society,* says that even an elaborate and well-
run youth program is not enough, for "the general body of
church members must never forget that they are ultimately
responsible for the education of the youth in their midst. They
must continually ask themselves: 'Are we the kind of church
that shows forth in its life the truth of God?' "[2]

*60. My teenager needs leadership, drive, and enthusiasm that
will attract him. Can the church offer this?*

This depends on the quality of life in the congregation. If
there is leadership, drive, and enthusiasm in the over-all life of
the local congregation, youngsters will be included and feel
accepted in the total group rather than simply within their
own youth group. This is perhaps most important about our
ministry to youth in the church: a feeling of at-homeness as
fully accepted members of the church. This is to be contrasted
with the feeling of many teenagers that the only place they
are really accepted is in an isolated Sunday-night group.

Many churches are concerned not only with the youth as a
special group but with the life of the congregation as a whole,
including children, youths, and adults. The attitudes that reflect this over-all concern mean that theirs is an educational
program from "womb to tomb." It is within this perspective
that any youth work is worth while.

Adolescents are seeking for a center for their lives. Their

dominant sentiment is emerging, the latent image of God is being developed, the integration of their personalities is taking place. In every boy and girl there is something to build on, and beyond every person there is something to build toward. If this growth does not center on Jesus Christ as the focal point of their lives, it will center somewhere else. There are always plenty of competitors for the loyalty of all the people and especially of young people. There is always the danger that young people will become disillusioned because somebody they admired let them down. Most skepticism probably is based on the experience of being hurt by someone who claims to be a Christian.

There is nothing radical to suggest for a youth program in the church. Many programs have worked for a time and then failed. Other programs that seem to fall below the standards of procedures recommended by the denominational head-quarters may work because of their attitude toward the youth as persons. Our responsibility is to love them enough to sense their real needs, be flexible enough to ride the waves, permit their own leadership to emerge in terms of their developing sense of responsibility, and stand by them as they make their own experiments.

As they explore all the possibilities of relating the Christian faith to their own lives, they are moving from elementary to advanced Christian teaching at their·own rate. They no longer need milk but solid food, for "solid food is for the mature, for those who have their faculties trained by practice to distinguish good from evil" (Hebrews 5:14, RSV). But they can accept this solid food from us only when they trust us.

61. *What does the church do to help our teenagers understand the problems of mixed marriages, especially between Protestants and Catholics?*

Almost every denomination has provided study guides to help young people think through this problem. In our mobile and pluralistic society, we must expect an increase in both

religiously and racially mixed marriages, and therefore youngsters need to know what is involved.

Even when such factors as cultural background, economic
values, family practices, and desire for children are shared
and enjoyed by two young people, differences in religion may
be so pronounced as to threaten the possibility of a successful
marriage. Sometimes this difficulty exists between two Protestants when their respective churches are opposed to each other.
There are both conservative and liberal approaches to Christianity that can create areas of conflict. This can be serious
not only religiously, but religion also dictates many of our
cultural and moral expectations.

In a Catholic–Protestant marriage, such differences are often
magnified. Again, it is partly a matter of conservative versus
liberal views of religious belief and practice, but it can lead
to differences about contraception, abortion, the number of
children, their baptism and religious training, and various
family practices. We have moved beyond the rigid restrictions
that Rome used to place on mixed marriages, so that the
wedding may be performed by a clergyman or a priest, no agree-
ments need to be signed, and the Catholic partner is not
excluded from communion in his church even if the wedding
ceremony has not been authorized by Catholic authorities.
However, the older practices often lead to unconscious pressures on the Protestant partner, who may feel guilty when
Protestant customs are followed in the home. In-laws, especially those with inherited antipathies toward either Protestants
or Catholics, may place pressures on one spouse or the other,
even going so far as to try to convert the children.

Sometimes this means that husband and wife do not worship together or have a common approach to religious practices
in the home. One or the other may take over the religious
nurture of the children, and therefore one parent is left out
and becomes a second-class citizen, at least in the eyes of
the children.

When religion becomes an area of conflict, one defense is

apathy. In order to place a proper emphasis on the person-to-person relations that make a family viable, both partners begin to drift away from their inherited religious practices, and the children receive no religious training.

But Catholic–Protestant marriages do work, and often they work well, no matter what the religious solution may be. If each spouse is secure in his or her faith and is tolerant of the faith of the other, there is little difficulty in working out a satisfactory solution to most of their problems. Or, in some cases where it may be done in good conscience, one spouse may convert to the other's religion or both may decide on a third common option.

A Catholic or Protestant may run into greater difficulties if the marriage is to a nonbeliever. Even when there is understanding and tolerance, the negative attitude of the nonbelieving spouse will be likely to corrode the faith of the believer, so that association with a church or the religious training of the children simply does not fit into the overall meaning of family life. The result may be a successful secular family life, or the other may change.

Our young people need to see what the problems are long before they become emotionally involved. Our churches are challenged to teach the tolerance characteristic of the American way of life in regard to those of different faiths and at the same time expected to buttress the faith of church members. By the time our young people are in high school, a few of them will have become so emotionally involved with those of other faiths that they will be unable to look at the problems. But in most cases this is the ideal time to face the situation. In most Protestant churches, Catholics are welcomed to the youth groups, and there are many opportunities to study the differences between their belief systems and practices and to point out how these work out in a marriage. Whenever possible, a Catholic priest or a Catholic–Protestant couple should be brought in as resource persons.

Success in marriage is a difficult achievement and needs all the support it can get. Religious, cultural, and racial differences may provide enrichment in many cases and become areas of conflict in others. And when young people make a decision, I believe that their parents should become supportive in a creative way.

62. *One of our sons wants to be a Christian minister. We think that he will be sacrificing too many good American values and that he can serve the church just as loyally as a lay person. How can we affect his vocational choice?*

This question reflects one of the most interesting twists in the thinking of Christian parents. If we can believe the historical records, the Christian ministry has for many years been considered by church people as a desirable vocation. Many parents have felt honored that one of their children has chosen to enter the Christian ministry and has been called in a very real sense to this specialized form of Christian service. In more recent years, however, statistics have shown that the average minister's salary is low, and many parents have felt that the choice of the ministry should be opposed. But seventy years ago when a young man wanted to go into the ministry, his father said to him, "Now, look, Ray, you have three brothers who are dentists and are making good money. If you want to go into the ministry and starve to death, that's your own business." In this particular case, Ray ended up with more money than his dentist brothers, but this was not the reason for his entering the ministry.

The ministry is not only a very high form of vocational service; it has many requirements and satisfactions not offered by other professions. It demands a high level of education, including three years of graduate work beyond college; it provides the advantage for working with people on a personal basis; it offers the opportunity to influence public opinion in many areas of life; it meets many people's need to feel that they are serving the Lord by helping others in many different ways; it demands a high degree of business sense and administrative skills in order to run a successful congregation as a business enterprise; and ultimately it means a life that is worth while in terms of ethical and moral standards.

The family life of the minister is not fragmented as much as that of people in many other occupations. If we can take seriously the findings in *Who's Who,* many ministers' children find their names in that volume because of the educational opportunities that are afforded them. Fewer divorces and family breakups occur among ministers. There is enough financial security to provide for satisfactory family living and resources for the education of the children. The life of a minister can become a great one in terms of the fundamental human values.

Of course, even parents who are active in the church may not see all of these values and satisfactions of the ordained ministry. They are likely to see the higher money values and higher social prestige that are attached to other vocations. They may not sense how demanding the ministry is in terms of skills and disciplines. Therefore, they are likely to say that the ministry should be avoided.

The implication underlying this question is that there is a ministry of the laity which is equally important. The power of the church lies in its lay ministry. The church lives in and affects the world around it through the ministry of lay people. The church as the people of God invades every level of work, education, and social and political activity, and each individual Christian has the opportunity to make his witness. There are two important things we can do in the church: keep the wrong people out of the ordained ministry; and emphasize the tremendous importance of the ministry of lay people. At this point parents are responsible for guiding their children into other vocations if they are not suited for the particular demands of the ordained ministry.

It is important for parents who stand in the way of a son's entering the ministry to examine their own motives as to why they are doing so.

63. *We would like our son to become a minister, but we don't want to push him unless he is really interested. How can*

we influence his early years so that he will naturally develop an interest in the ministry? Can we do this without his being aware of it?

The answer to this question is the other side of the coin of the previous question. The parent's job is never to push a boy into a particular vocation, whether it be what his father has done, or what his father wishes he had done, or an occupation that is idealized. The most that we can hope for is to expose a child to the possibilities of various vocations, of which the ministry is one. If a boy has the aptitudes that make possible the development of the appropriate skills, he should have the opportunity and the discipline that will move him in this direction.

A young boy who shows skill at the piano should have every opportunity to develop this skill at an early age. The parents may find that they have to stimulate the child, but at the same time they must be prepared to allow him to forsake this skill if it doesn't interest him. Mickey Mantle is said to have become a great baseball player because his father began playing baseball with him at an early age. But if Mickey Mantle had not had the aptitudes to do what his father was not able to do, or had not developed the interest in becoming a baseball player, even all of these opportunities to play baseball at an early age would not have led him to the high level of development that he has reached. Many boys develop skills because of their aptitudes and because of their ability to find among their acquaintances certain models they wish to follow.

If I wanted my boy to be a minister, it would be the last thing that I would tell him. What I would hope for is that in the normal development of his personality and in his increasing devotion as a Christian he would come across those ministers who might become models for him. He would have opportunities to make decisions as his education proceeded, and in time he would make his own decision as to what vocation he wished to enter. In this case, I would be pleased if he decided on the ministry, but, at the same time, I would not think he had chosen something lower in the Christian scale of values if he decided on any other job.

It is most important for one to find the job that does justice to his aptitudes, that meets the needs of the society around him, and that contributes to the betterment of the world. Any job that meets these three requirements is a possible Christian vocation.

CHAPTER VII

The Family and the Church

64. I want our family to become a Christian family: this is why I go to official board meetings and men's clubs, my wife belongs to women's and missionary societies, and Johnny and Carol attend youth-group meetings. But now we don't see each other any more.

Some churches manage to divide families, although this is certainly not their intention. In order to meet the needs of individuals, many churches have various organizations for men, women, young people, and children; and in order to insure a smooth-running organization, these meetings are scattered throughout the week. It is possible for members of a church-related family to attend as individuals some meeting every night of the week, therefore having no opportunity to establish the organic unity of the family which is essential to living together as Christians.

One young mother asked her minister which organizations she should join and was shocked at his reply: "I don't think you should join any organization. Your job as a Christian is to be at home with your small children." This church did provide a special nursery for small children at a time when father and mother attended parents' classes together, but this was all they were expected to do in the church.

65. Isn't religion just for children? Why should we have to go to church with them?

Very few parents phrase their question in this way, but by their behavior they show their answer to the question. Their feeling is that they should *send* their children to Sunday School and when they are old enough to quit, fine. After all, the parents quit when they reached high school age and have not seen fit to return to church since then, except maybe to be married and to go on Christmas and Easter. These are the parents who devotedly chauffeur their children to Sunday School on Sunday mornings and pick them up afterward. A cartoon on the front of a *New Yorker* showed fathers in their shirt sleeves sitting in their cars outside the church reading the sports section while the children were getting their weekly dose of religion. This is a caricature of the Christian faith, but all too often it actually works out this way.

Religion is primarily for adults. The Bible is an adult book. The goal of Christian faith is a level of maturity impossible for children to achieve. The decisions demanded by God's claim on us are the responsible choices of Christian freedom. Adults who do not have children find the activities of the church an important element in their lives.

Many adults have drifted away from the church. As parents, this means that they are failing in their responsibility to themselves and their children. But if they have accepted the Christian interpretation of parental vocation, they need to bring the family-as-a-unit into the organic fellowship of church life. This is impossible if they send their children to church but remain indifferent themselves. The church today is beginning to see more clearly that families must have an opportunity to be together in church on Sundays, and parents find that in response to this they strengthen not only their own parenthood but also their adult faith in Christianity.

66. Our Sunday School wants us to attend family worship with our children and also go to a special class. This seems like a lot to demand of us.

If what we have been saying throughout this book about

the nature of the Christian family is to be taken seriously, it involves the relation of the family-as-a-unit to the ongoing life of the local congregation. Some parents think this is a tremendous demand on them, but other parents welcome this opportunity. Only a very few churches have said that if you do not register with your child, your child may not attend Sunday School. However, in such churches, there is 100 per cent co-operation of parents and children attending the family worship together, with the parents going to classes that are tied in with what their children are learning. This is an extreme form of coercion on the part of the church, but it works. One church that tried this system had a limited enrollment because of its facilities, and had a waiting list for a number of years.

If a church takes seriously this problem of the relation of the parents to the children in the church, the parents will respond. If, however, only the formal requirement is made and nothing vital happens to either the parents or the children, such a program deservedly will fail.

Many questions have been asked about a family-oriented service of worship and here are some of the answers:

a. Who goes to the family service?

The whole family. Babies in arms or in buggies attend with their brothers and sisters and parents and even grandparents. Not everyone will stay all the way through, but they all start together. Local conditions dictate when the younger ones leave.

b. What time is the service held?

Early enough to allow time for a genuine service of worship and an adequate class period. The best arrangement is to start at 9:00 or 9:15 a.m. The service lasts about thirty to forty minutes, and then everyone goes to class until 10:45. The period of worship is long enough to make an unhurried use of the traditional service as adapted and to permit a fifty-minute class period, which is the minimum time for adequate teaching.

c. What follows the family service?

Classes for everyone. When the children go to their classes, so do the parents. The parents' class is the heart of the program, for until the parents understand what is being accomplished through the total process, they are unable to provide the assist-ance that is needed. The parents' class asks two fundamental questions: (1) What is the meaning of the Christian faith to me as a parent? (2) How can I be a mediator of the Gospel to my children where they are? Books such as Reuel L. Howe's *Man's Need and God's Action* have been used as texts, but the class should be primarily a discussion group led by a husband and wife team, with an adequate resource leader present.

Of course, because the whole parish is a family, most con-gregations will have classes for adults who are not parents. Bible classes and other types of adult study groups (as distinct from parents with their special needs) operate within the sys-tem. In larger parishes, there may be many classes of parents with about twenty to a class.

d. What use do parents make of the family service in class?

Children and their parents often come from the family service full of questions about the experience they have just had (which is why the family service comes first, and cannot be the 11:00 a.m. service). These questions are often the self-starters of the class session. Usually the topic leads into a planned session for the day, but there is good reason for spending a few minutes relating the experiences of worship to the daily lives of the pupils, no matter what the lesson plan says. This is as true of the children's classes as of the parents' discussion. Teachers and parents are helped when they receive in advance the hymns and lessons for the coming months.

All of this becomes grist for the mill in discussion at home. No parent has to ask what happened in church school!

e. How is the family service modified to meet the needs of all?

The family service should be enough like the traditional 11:00 a.m. service to enable a child to feel at home in both, but the family service ministers to the family-as-a-unit and recognizes the limits of the attention span and intellectual capacity of the children. The simplicity of this service often captures the loyalty of parents, especially of fathers who dislike more formal presentations.

The success of the service depends on the relevance of the selections, the tempo of the service, and the reverence of the adults. If it drags or gets too long, the children become restless.

f. What lessons are read from the Bible?

Selection must be made in terms of the unity and theme of the service. Care must be taken to find the point of relevance and to make it clear before the reading begins. Many ministers find that modern translations, such as the Smith-Goodspeed Complete Bible, the Revised Standard Version, the New English Bible, and the Phillip's translation of the New Testament, communicate the Gospel to both the children and their parents more effectively than does the King James version.

g. What kind of sermon should be preached?

The purpose is to proclaim the Gospel so that the congregation will hear it. Some preachers effectively work out an exposition of the Bible story to children, but the problem is to make it relevant to the current situation. Many modern stories about real children which parallel the Bible story are often more suitable. Imagination, humor, the light touch, and a genuine understanding of the problems facing the congregation are essential.

The informality of the service offers an opportunity for questions, quizzes, and contests. Occasionally either the children or the parents can be told to stop listening because the next point is for the other group. In 1869, Horace Bushnell preached a sermon entitled "God's Thoughts Fit Bread for Children," and toward the end he said, "I think I see it now clearly: we do not preach well to adults, because we do not preach, or learn how to preach, to children. Jesus did not forget to be a child; but if he had been a child with us, we should probably have missed the sight of him."

h. What hymns do we sing?

The family service should have a small repertoire of about sixty hymns. These should provide a balance between the classical hymns of the church and the best of the children's hymns. One of the most satisfactory systems is to use a very simple opening hymn for two or three Sundays, giving the information to the teachers and parents in advance so that nonreaders may memorize either the refrain or one stanza of the hymn. Thus the very youngest children can participate verbally in a portion of the service. The other hymns later in the service may be of a more advanced kind.

Most hymnals are full of hymns suitable to families, although there are few hymns about families. Every church should learn the new hymn by F. Bland Tucker, the first stanza of which is

> "Our Father, by whose Name
> All fatherhood is known,
> Who dost in love proclaim
> Each family thine own,
> Bless thou all parents, guarding well,
> With constant love as sentinel,
> The homes in which thy people dwell."[1]

i. When should we have baptisms or dedications?

In churches that practice either infant baptism or infant dedication, this act should be part of public worship, and the family service is ideal for it. On such Sundays, everyone stays, even the youngest children. Usually the order of service is changed. After the opening hymn, the story or sermonette should be on the meaning of baptism, with some words addressed to the parents. Then a special baptismal hymn may be sung prior to the actual service, which might include a Bible lesson on either Jesus' attitudes to children or his own baptism. After the baptism the service may conclude with prayers, birthday offering, offering, Doxology, and closing hymn. The children in the church should be placed where they can see the baby, child, or adult being baptized; and adults might well be seated at this point, with the children standing.

j. What does this do to the 11:00 a.m. service?

In most cases it makes very little difference. Some parents and children stay through the entire morning. Baby-sitting service is provided for younger children at 11:00. But the family service *is* church!

What usually happens is that the family service shows a gain in attendance, chiefly from parents who would not or could not come at 11:00 anyway. A new congregation is born without hurting the other one. They come together for many combination services, with various choirs singing together, at Thanksgiving, Christmas, Easter, and Pentecost. The congregation as a whole becomes a true family of God. This fellowship of the Holy Spirit discovers itself to be a true church through its worship, and the effects are seen in parish life and throughout the community.

Family nights and other ways of ministering to the family-as-a-unit are discovered, and the children know that they are members of the congregation of Christ's flock. They also discover that they are members of Christian families because they go to church with Mother and Dad.

67. *We have been told that our children's image of God will reflect their image of us as parents. How can the church help us to fill this seemingly impossible role of God?*

Psychologically the parents are God to the infant and small child. This is why the early years of a child's life are so important religiously and why the parents are the chief ministers during this period. By the time a child is three, however, he begins to see that these parental idols have clay feet. If the parents then are able to admit that they are not all-wise and all-powerful and all-good, but are normal human beings, the children will soon realize that their faith is not in their parents but in their parents' faith. The one God who is perfect is the God who is worshiped by their parents. This period lasts until the child is in his teens and is ready to make his own decision about the reality of the Living God.

This role is not difficult for parents to accept if they can point beyond themselves to the God in whom they believe. If they have no belief in a power beyond themselves, however, the child may develop either a humanistic faith or a creeping disillusionment. This is why it is important for parents to admit their failings to their children under the proper circumstances, to go to church with their children so that they may see them participating in a prayer of confession, and to make clear that they, like their children, have need of God's grace. The purpose of the parents in the last analysis is not to be God but to be a channel of grace so that the Living God may work through them, and this is primarily a problem of interpersonal relationships on a purely human level.

68. How can I convince Victor that he should go to Sunday School alone, without getting myself involved? Like most suburban parents, we don't want to be pillars of the church; we just want to attend occasionally. Is there any way of using and contributing to the church without marrying it?

Too much activity in the church by members of the family as individuals may interfere with family life. However, there is a distinction between becoming too involved in church work and doing the work of the church in our lives. Unless there is a degree of involvement on the part of the parents, the children are not likely to take Sunday School seriously. The parents' attitude toward the church must be different from their attitude toward the school or toward the various Scout and other groups in which their children participate. The Christian faith is not primarily for children but for adults.

Because it is primarily the parents' faith that influences the children, the parents' involvement in the life of the church is the most crucial issue of all. We cannot use the church and buy its privileges. Rather, we must become involved in the church sufficiently to recognize God's claim on us in our role as parents and as citizens. There is simply no way to escape this if we are going to do the right job. This does not mean that parents have to be Sunday School teachers or join various other organizations, but it does mean that they need to be involved consistently in the worshiping life of a congregation and in the ongoing educational program. How much more they do beyond this is a matter of their own needs and inclinations.

69. *I can't enjoy life when everybody in the family is either mad at each other or running off in a different direction. Can the church help us to enjoy family life together?*

This is basically a question about the family rather than about the church. The church can provide guidance for family life in the many ways we have been discussing in this chapter, but the fundamental problem of the organic unity of the family in overcoming difficulties and misunderstandings and in finding things that can be enjoyed together is a matter of family decision.

It is at this point that many families discover the significance of a family council or family discussion in which they can share their problems and interests together. Here is the opportunity for facing difficulties, acquiring patience, and working out satisfactory solutions. The success of such an undertaking of course depends upon the attitudes within the family.

When each member of the family realizes and accepts the fact that all should be concerned with the welfare of each, there is room for a great deal of individual activity. There is no reason why families should do everything together, for in many cases what is important is for each person to follow his own aptitudes and interests backed by the concern of the other members of the family. Genuine family unity allows the freedom of individual action *and* the sharing of interests with all the others in the family.

70. *How does religion as an additional activity in our family's life lead us to a more honest and deep relation with one another?*

Religion to be taken on as an extra burden is not likely to contribute much to family life. It is more helpful to recognize that the Christian faith may be an *integral* part of family life. This implies an understanding of the fundamental meaning of the marriage and family from the perspective of the Christian faith. Marriage is here viewed as a relationship between man and woman based primarily on love. This love is a combination of the possessiveness of strong attachment, the sense of companionship and community, and the self-giving love of which the New Testament speaks. These three types of love are usually intermixed in every marriage. A marriage is based on mutual consent and is consummated by the sex relationship. D. S. Bailey, an English authority on the meaning of marriage, writes that "the true, authentic *henosis* is affected by intercourse following consent between a man and a woman who love one another and who act freely, deliberately, responsibly, and with the knowledge and approval of the community, and in so doing (whether they know it or not) conform to the Divine law."[2]

This husband-wife relationship is primary, and out of it comes the presence of children and the creation of the family. The family is a fellowship of parents and children achieved through the interweaving of interests so that all members are free to develop their potentials. In and through these shared interests based on love, God is at work whether they know it or not.

God therefore is the hub of family life, and religion, if it is taken seriously, is not one more added activity but is the center of the love that holds the family together.

This cohesiveness of the family is supported by the church and its activities. This common reliance on God is what makes possible the honest and deep relations in the family. This is not something superadded but something which emerges. It involves hard work and willingness to sacrifice on the part of every member of the family, and it means that at all times the channels of communications are kept open. If and when barriers arise, it is possible through repentance and forgiveness to reopen the channels and therefore to maintain the relationships on the deepest possible level. This is the glory of Christian family life.

71. How can we get our church to set up a family program?
It seems to me that the church divides families.

The starting point in getting the whole congregation to minister to the family-as-a-unit is what attitudes are shared by the believers. Many congregations are ready for this step when they see what is involved, and others are satisfied with things as they are. Unless they have already discovered the nature of the church as a community of the Holy Spirit, they are not likely to see the family as a cell of the larger body. The local congregation needs to discover the church's concern to strengthen the intimacy of family life and its foundations in terms of the love of God working through interpersonal relationships.

The factor of motivation is primary. In some parishes, it may begin with the trustees or the vestry or whatever the ruling body is called. In other cases, it may begin with the development of policy in the parish council or the committee on religious education. In other congregations, it may arise from the parents' challenging the church to minister to them as a unit. In some churches, it may come from a small group of people who have gained this insight in another parish and seek to bring about similar changes in the parish of which they are now members.

Some churches discover that this demand is placed upon them because of the kind of materials they are using in the Sunday School. The United Presbyterian Church U.S.A., the United Church of Christ, and the Protestant Episcopal Church have been in the forefront in insisting on parental co-operation in the educational program. *The Seabury Series* of the Episcopal Church has gone the farthest in insisting on family worship, classes for parents, and the kind of leadership training that makes possible effective teaching of children and adults alike.

In some churches the pastor may be the bottleneck. Either because of a lack of inclination or a lack of training, he may resist such radical changes in the church's program and may need to be persuaded by personal discussion, pressure from the teachers and parents, or a change in policy of the committee on

Christian education. Sometimes he may be helped by taking the opportunity to read such books as J. C. Wynn's *Pastoral Ministry to Families* (Philadelphia: Westminster Press; 1958), Charles Kean's *The Christian Gospel in the Parish Church* (Greenwich: The Seabury Press; 1953), or my *Education for Christian Living* (Englewood Cliffs, N.J.: Prentice-Hall, Inc.; 1956).

When churches are convinced of the adequacy of this program, it is important to begin by setting up a family service. Sometimes this may be held on Christmas or Easter, or once a month, before it becomes a full-fledged weekly program. Some churches need to face the problem of multiple services, double sessions of church school classes, and even the distance of the parish house from the church.

The parents' class is the key problem. It should not deal with adult problems alone. Leadership may come from those parents who have already developed skills in directing a discussion, even if they cannot pose as experts in the field. Resource persons may be called in to provide information as it is needed, or members may obtain the information from books and report to the class. The agenda for discussion may emerge from the family service, from a listing of problems and questions, or from manuals especially prepared for parents' classes. Some classes have a permanent leader who qualifies as an expert. Each class will develop its own way of doing things through experimentation.

CHAPTER VIII

Religious Questions
and Parents' Responsibilities

72. *How do I answer my six-year-old child when he asks, "Who is God and where does he live?"*

One six-year-old boy was heard to say, "God is in my stomach and he is dead." Having been taught that God is a spirit inside us and that Jesus had died on the Cross, he quite naturally confused things. This points to the difficulty of interpreting God in any verbal way to children of an early age.

First, we need to realize that, as children are bound to hear the word "God," they are likely to ask this fundamental question. If the parents are determined not to discuss God, the children will hear about him from their playmates or at school. Therefore, it is essential that parents have some idea of what they mean by God before they try to interpret him to their children.

Second, we need to make clear to the child that there are many different ideas about God and the word is not one that can be easily understood. No one has ever seen God, and therefore we are dealing with someone who is invisible and about whom there has been a great deal of confused discussion. Even a six-year-old can be told that different people in all parts of the world hold various conceptions of God. He may even be introduced to some of the strange ideas of God that are found in the Old Testament.

Third, we need to try to relate the idea of God to experiences that children can understand. Sometimes we can relate it to the giving of life as we see it in the birth of animals. God as the "Lord and Giver of Life" can lie behind our interpretation of nature, of the birth of a new baby, or of plants growing in the fields. It is no accident that little children sing "The little flowers come through the ground at Easter time." A six-year-old can also begin to understand something of the laws of nature and to see the hand of God behind the order of stars and the laws of nature. The six- or-seven-year-old may be very much interested in astronomy and in the fact that comets appear at certain specific times that can be predicted. The accuracy of our astronomical knowledge is a great asset in understanding the orderliness of God's universe.

Fourth, we can stress the fact that God works through love relationships. The child can understand that God is love at work through the relationships in the family, that God is at work when we forgive each other.

Fifth, children will hear the word "God" used in ways that are outside their experience. Often this is simply the sense of the mysterious and the holiness of a transcendent God, and this cannot be explained so much as it can be felt; where it arouses a sense of awe or wonder at the mysteriousness of God, it can be good. Sometimes, however, it can lead to a dangerous type of thinking, as in the case of the child who said, "God killed Jesus." There is also the danger that God will be thought of as a kind of Pollyanna, so that our kindergarten interpretation of nature is such that we do not see the "dog eat dog" aspect of the life around us. The child must gain an idea of God that does not ignore the conflicts and the suffering and the fear and the anger existing in his world.

An unrealistic concept of God may endanger a child's life. Three-year-old Sally wandered from her back yard down through the trees to a stream and was standing there on the rocks. She had never gone there before because she had been closed in her yard, but a gate had been left open. Her mother found her standing on a rock precariously near the edge overlooking the stream. If she had fallen in, the water would have swept her away. The mother was both scared and angry and asked Sally why she went there. "Didn't you know you might have drowned?" The child's answer was very simple: "You told me that God would take care of me. If I fell, God would pick me up; and if I started to drown, God would save me." Here the idea of God's loving care had been so interpreted that it became a very dangerous element in Sally's life and could have caused her death. Some parents who have heard this story have responded with the phrase, "Wasn't that sweet?" Other parents have responded, with more realism and Christian faith, "It was terrible to teach a child such an unrealistic concept of God!"

We need to avoid the idea of God as a celestial policeman, or as a miracle worker, or as one who makes people good, or as one who makes people afraid. Let us be sure that the concepts we share with our children are such that as they grow older they will never need to unlearn them. They are going to have many mistaken notions that need to be corrected, but there is no reason why parents should contribute to these misconceptions by watered-down views of God or erroneous ideas that sound cute because they are for children. We need to avoid abstract and complicated interpretations because children think in con-crete and simple terms. But at the same time we must never make them feel that the answers about God are easy to come by.

Much depends on the parents' capacity to discern the work of God in daily events. Mary Alice Jones tells of a conversation between Bobby and his mother. Bobby had planted a radish that did not grow because he had not watered it, and he was annoyed because God did not water his garden for him. Finally his mother asked:

"Do you think it would be a good plan if he did? If he treated you as if you were baby Mary, who has to have every-thing done for her?"

"I would not like to be treated like the baby," Bobby decided. "I should have remembered to water my garden."[1]

Bobby had learned about his own responsibility in terms of God's order in the world.

73. *How can I teach my child about the Bible without giving him false notions of God, creation, miracles, and the world of science?*

In the first place, the Bible is an adult book. It was written over a long period of time by the most competent seers of the Jews and Christians and was edited and rearranged by the responsible leaders of both faiths. It is not an easy book even for adults. It is a book of profound significance, sacred to Jews and Christians alike, and is essential to the continued religious growth of both children and adults.

Over the years, the Bible has been subjected to more intensive study than any other book. It has been analyzed scientifically, historically, linguistically, and theologically. To some people it is simply the history of a religious community. To others it is the story of salvation. To others it is a record of man's search for God that has not been entirely successful. To others it is literally and word for word a revelation of what God has said to us. To others it is the story of the drama of redemption, a record of God's mighty acts in history, which is open to interpretation in terms of modern scientific study.

What the parent teaches his children about the Bible depends upon his own point of view. He needs to decide what he thinks about the Bible as well as what he believes to be the capacity of his children to grasp the Bible's meaning. In facing this problem, he needs to become aware of many erroneous views. The Bible is sometimes considered so sacred that it is looked on as an idol: it is to be treated with reverence, as we treat our flag, and may become a symbol of one's devotion even if the book is never opened. At the other extreme, superstitious ideas about the Bible may be reflected in such statements as "If I drop the Bible, I will die," or, "If I have the Bible in my pocket I will not be shot by an enemy soldier." The Bible in this case becomes a talisman of good or bad luck. Some people think that all parts of the Bible have equal value, and therefore it makes no difference what part is studied in terms of understanding God's revelation. In other cases, particularly in our Sunday Schools, selections are made from the Bible in terms of what will interest the children regardless of religious value. Many Bible stories are taught without regard to the religious issues facing children.

It is important to remember that the Bible was written over a long period of time by a great number of people and that it consists not only of the sixty-six books but of many other sources which have been combined by editors to reduce it to this number. It is a great library rather than a single book. It is the literature of the people of God, both Jews and Christians, and has been a means of insight into the nature of God for many generations. The variety of literature covers history, moral teachings, miracle stories, legends, myths, poetry, law, sermons, and parables. There may be others, but this is enough to indicate the variety of religious literature we find.

We can read the Bible for many reasons: to find out what other people have thought; to evaluate certain kinds of behavior; to discover ways in which God has forgiven, redeemed, and pronounced judgment on individuals, nations, and ultimately all mankind. We can find many characters in the Bible with whom we can identify. Some of these are heroes whom we admire, many more are people very much like us, and some are utterly despicable. But all of them lived under God whether they knew it or not.

In my *Biblical Theology and Christian Education* I have tried to spell out the meaning of the Bible for today by calling it a drama of redemption. As a record of God's mighty acts in history with this world as the stage, we divide the drama into five acts. The story begins with creation, followed by a covenant, reaches a climax with the coming of Christ, continues into the story of the church (and this is the point at which we enter the drama), and points toward the consummation or end of it all. Study of the Bible within this framework gives us a point of perspective whereby we may relate these stories to our own lives. We believe that God is at work in the historical process and that his purpose is to reconcile the world to him. God is seeking to save us from sin and separation, from loneliness and frustration, from anxiety and withdrawal. In and through the life of the church, which lives by this biblical faith, we find that we are drawn from our selfish and ego-centered way into a life of service of God and man. If the parents understand and accept this point of view, they may communicate the Bible in a relevant way to their children.

The beginning point in the teaching of the Bible is not in using its words. A small child needs to be exposed to the biblical faith of his parents through the relationships of family life. If we look at the five acts of the drama of God at work in history, we discover that every child needs what the biblical faith has to offer. The child has been created by his father and mother, and we as Christians believe this to be the work of God through the biological expression of love. The child may in some cases be the result of an act of lust, and thus, at the very moment of his creation, personal relationships determine what will happen to him. The point is that he has experienced creation, much as Adam and Eve did, and immediately faces a world in which he may or may not be loved and may or may not respond favorably. How the parents treat him at this moment determines what creation means to him.

A little child first becomes acquainted with natural law at the point of accepting or rejecting food, in terms of whether he is hurt or not, in terms of the way in which he is cared for; and he comes up against moral law in terms of the dependability of his parents. At this point he is in a covenant relationship with his parents and through them with God. The laws of God apply to him from the moment of birth. The Ten Commandments are valid whether he knows it or not.

Sooner or later in his early days he will experience rejection owing to his parents' thoughtlessness or anger or impatience and will therefore become anxious. In the case of an unwanted child, this rejection may occur at birth and affect his will to live. But in most families, the child will experience reconciliation. There is no guarantee that this will happen, but most parents express their love in ways that draw the child back into the family community after he has been rejected.

Many families also demonstrate this love of God by having a child baptized or dedicated and brought into the life of the church. Thus from the very beginning the child with his parents are part of the larger community of faithful people. Oftentimes, however, this is merely a token acceptance of the demands of society, and the baptism, like some vaccinations, doesn't take and therefore does not become the channel of God's grace for the child or his parents.

Furthermore even the new-born infant faces the consummation. Infants do die. Through the ministry of his parents he faces the judgment of God. The point is, the new-born child is within the drama of redemption as told in the Bible from the moment of his birth. With a small baby, very few, if any, words can be used to express more than the emotional tone of this biblical faith.

Within this framework of the drama of redemption, it is possible to communicate the meaning of the Bible to every age level. The Bible gives us the idea of a living God, who is Lord of history and at work in and through human relationships. This idea of God is open to constant re-examination in the light of our knowledge of modern science, because we do not make our idea of God dependent upon a particular world view. The story of creation, for example, so important for understanding the biblical story, is not a literal interpretation of what happened but is the product of the Hebrew imagination. It is more like poetry and is rich in its possible interpretations for the meaning of life. It is important for the child of seven or eight, as he hears the story, to realize that there are two different accounts of creation. The opening account in the first chapter of Genesis was written some four hundred years after the earlier story of Adam and Eve in the second chapter. The two stories fit together surprisingly well but emphasize different aspects and at some points contradict each other. We do not expect scientific accuracy and consistency in these early folk tales. It is sometimes helpful to portray these stories as having come down from generation to generation passed by word of mouth around the camp fires of a wandering people and only later written down. The amazing thing is that even today as we read this story it speaks in such a way that God is revealed to us and we understand better our relationship to him.

We may have more trouble with the miracle stories, depending upon our current interpretation of the miraculous. The Bible speaks to a world view far different from ours. What seemed miraculous to the Bible writers might very well today be a fact of astronomy or medicine or psychiatry. At the same time, we cannot simply dismiss miracles, because we hear reports of them even in the twentieth century. There are wonderful stories of recoveries from illness, of recovery even from death through the miracle of heart massage, of encounters with people who seem to be guided by an outside force. Many of these instances may be interpreted as pure chance or as the work of God, but certainly they are not the events that might be predicted in the light of our current knowledge of the world. What we have the right to do, it seems to me, is to take each of the miracle stories of the Bible and to ask why it was written, what it reveals about the nature of God, and finally whether or not this event really occurred as described or grew up as a means of interpreting the nature of God to the people. The raising of Lazarus, for example, seems improbable on the face of it, but if what is being communicated here is the fact that new life can come out of death, it fits into the total scheme of things, not as fact, but as an acted parable. Certainly the story of the Ascension is in this same category of being an account within the framework of a three-storied universe of a genuine experience of the apostles. The apostles did cease at some point to be aware of the presence of the Risen Lord, and the story is told in terms of what might be called a "flying saucer theology." Literally the story is absurd to children and adults alike, but what is being said through the story is very important.

The science of biblical times is far removed from the science of today. Therefore we expect such primitive literature to reflect its own scientific insights. The belief in demons in the New Testament was consistent with the psychology of that period. Today the phenomena described are open to current psychiatric investigations and it is possible to come to conclusions about the symptoms and the disease. The point is not that demons vanished into the swine but that a man was cured of his emotional distress. We can accept our space age and develop our theology accordingly without discarding the fundamental revelation of God which we find in the Bible. Thinking these things through is difficult but not impossible for children or adults.

Our task is to help our children face these questions from the very beginning. When a child says "Is it really true?" or "Did it actually happen?" he is asking a question in terms of empirical description. If he asks a question reflecting doubts concerning the nail holes in Jesus' hands, his question means this: "If I had been there, could I have put my fingers in physical holes in the hands?" The child or young person is willing to make distinctions between empirical descriptions, myths, poetry, and even the prescientific attempts at describing experience. But he wants to know which is which. This is the point at which the parents' and teachers' honesty is at stake. They need to understand something of the relation of the critical faculties of the mind to religious faith. Many lay people feel that to ask such questions is to threaten the faith. Actually seeking the answers to such questions will clarify one's faith and therefore free us to act as Christians in the world without intellectual misgivings. This is why we read books written by experts about the Bible. They can give us information that we cannot get by ourselves. If these problems are faced clearly at all times, and especially if they are brought to the attention of our junior high school children, whether they are asking the questions or not, we can clear the decks for critical and constructive religious thinking by our teenagers.

Often our problem is finding the religious value of what is

preted. The letters of Paul, especially, take for granted that Jesus is remembered, emphasize that he is known still as the Risen Lord, and then is interpreted in great detail.

The mistake that parents and teachers often make is either to confuse the teachings about Jesus with the teachings about God, so that Jesus is not seen to be a man at all, or to emphasize Jesus as a nice man to the extent that there is no way of understanding him as Lord. This problem is sufficiently complicated to confuse adults, so we cannot expect children to grasp the solution easily. I have tried to spell this out in a brief book called *I Remember Jesus* (Greenwich: The Seabury Press, 1958), in which a picture of Jesus is provided for both young people and adults that will at least be a start in the direction of interpretation. I have listed at the end of Chapter IX a number of books which will be helpful to parents interpreting Jesus to their children.

74. *What shall I tell my child about death?*

The fact of death rises up and strikes children when they are completely unprepared for it. Because the adult attitude toward death is very often that of uncertainty, doubt, or refusal to face the event, many of us are incapable of preparing our children for the loss of loved ones. Because adults do not always realize what a shock death is to children's security, they may tell them the wrong things.

A child's father dies and he is told, "Daddy's gone away." The child expects his daddy to come back soon. When the child's father does not return, other deceptions are necessary and a belated facing of death is inevitable. But this period of uncertainty for the child coupled with his loss of faith in the adults on whom he depends is worse than the shock of death. Another child is told that his mommy is "in the ground," with no religious interpretation of life after death.

Contrasted with a "hush-hush" attitude toward death and the refusal to face facts are the experiences children have as they watch motion pictures and television. In the course of one evening of mystery stories on TV they may be exposed to ten different types of homicide, several fatal accidents, and perhaps a few natural deaths. There are no interpretations of these deaths. Both bad and good people come to sudden ends, usually without compassion and almost always without faith.

The child gradually becomes aware of death, even before he begins watching movies and TV. He may hear of death in family conversations or be faced with it among people he knows. The child who says, almost in agony, "Don't die, Mommy," is aware that his security rests in the continuing physical presence of his mother. Out of this awareness comes the conviction that he, too, will die someday. By the time he is six, he has some degree of fear of his own death, sometimes suggested by "If I should die before I wake" or some other childhood prayer.

As a child gets older, the more direct are his experiences of death. Perhaps it is a pet that dies; goldfish and turtles do not last long. Dogs that are loved with a great passion are hit by cars or are poisoned. Older people keep dying regularly, including beloved grandparents, great aunts and uncles, and neighbors. He sees the hearse come next door. Perhaps he must face the death, by disease or accident, of friends his own age. He may lose a brother or a sister. In more cases than we like to think of, fathers and mothers die when children are young.

We cannot escape the fact of death, no matter how young the child may be. The Christian Gospel has a great message of faith in the face of the certainty that all men die. "In the midst of life we are in death." "Man, that is born of a woman, hath but a short time to live. . . . He cometh up, and is cut down like a flower; he fleeth as it were a shadow, and never continueth in one stay" (Job 14:1–2). In accord with this realistic view of death, there is the Christian answer, "From henceforth blessed are the dead who die in the Lord; even so saith the Spirit; for they rest from their labors" (Rev. 14:13).

How we approach the problem of death with children depends primarily on two factors: first, our faith in life after death; second, our view of the needs of children as they face the fact of death.

Our view of death arises from our theology, our beliefs. We know that God made us and he saw that his creation was good, that in man's freedom men fall from grace, and that in God's providence all men die. We also have the hope of everlasting life through faith in Jesus Christ. Perhaps the best statement of this faith is found in Paul's letter to the Corinthians, in which he says, "Flesh and blood cannot inherit the kingdom of God," but there is a "spiritual body," and "this mortal must put on immortality" (I Cor. 15:50, 44, 53).

Our approach to the problem of death will come naturally from the experiences and questions of children. If we are willing to explain simply and honestly what happens in death, and then give them a sense of our own assurance of life after death, they can avoid the fears and superstitions that may be ruinous to their personalities.

If we are fortunate, the first questions will arise from the death of a pet. Here is an opportunity for sympathy in the face of loss. The child may wish to have a simple burial. Most of us assume that there is no immortality for animals. Thus the center of our concern will be the realistic acceptance of death and sympathy in the face of loss. This is valuable because it offers an opportunity to experience the fact of death without the overtones of hope, and yet it prepares the ground for understanding the difference between the death of an animal and the death of a human being in a child's mind.

When we face human death, we must keep our explanations in proper perspective. The child can see the dead body; he can watch a casket being lowered into the ground. If we leave him there, he is lost. But he is capable of one basic question: "What about the part I can't see?" He can say, "Daddy's body is in the ground, but the part I love is with God." He can distinguish between body and spirit, and therefore knows what Paul meant when he said, "There is a physical body, and there is a spiritual body" (I Cor. 15:44).

Not only do honest and simple explanations help, but the resources of the child's experiences in the church are available. From the time a child is three, he is exposed to the services of the church at Easter. This glorious event has such accessories as rabbits and flowers. However, the central theme is the Risen Christ who is victorious over death and who is living for us. The child may be too young to understand the words, but he can sense the importance of Easter Day through the drama and music. As he gets older and as the explanations become more adequate, the events are placed in their proper historical setting and he shares in the worship of the risen and historical Christ.

By all means let a child attend funerals, especially those which are not going to be excessively emotional. In church funerals, the congregation participates in hymns of victory and makes the responses in worship, and the child will sense something of the faith of the Christian community. I have never forgotten the experience of watching a family marching out of a church behind a casket singing, "Onward Christian Soldiers."

Death dislocates the lives of children more than adults suspect. Children should be prepared for this with all the resources of Christian hope. They need the ministry of the church in times of tragedy. Words and a pat on the head will not suffice, for their basic human relationships are broken by death, and only richer relationships of love will suffice to heal the wounds and bind up the broken-hearted. The whole congregation must learn to minister to children in their bereavement by providing the steadiness of routine, the sense of security, and the dependableness that they have lost through death. No evasion or sentimentality or misguided theology will help; these things stunt children's spiritual growth. Superficial pious words can destroy their faith. They need the true hope that resides in faith in Christ, and they can find this only as we minister to their real needs.

75. *How can I help my six-year-old child overcome fear of the dark, of punishment, of war?*

Fear of the dark may develop quite suddenly for any number of reasons. Most of these have to do with the loss of a sense of security owing to some kind of accidental occurrence, the comments of other children, or the child's sudden realization that he may die. Death is associated with darkness. Sometimes we can get at this fear of the dark by rooting out the cause, but often the only thing we can do is deal with the symptom. It is most important to provide an atmosphere of greater security. Sometimes what the child needs most is more time with his mother or father at bedtime; sometimes simple reassurance will be enough, sometimes prayers will help, and sometimes the only answer is to leave the light on until the child has gone to sleep. The important thing to recognize is that fear of the dark is not something abnormal but that it is rooted in some cause which in time will eliminate itself.

Fear of punishment is often the result of the way in which parents and others administer punishment. If a child has developed a tremendous sense of guilt and has an over-sensitive conscience, he may come to fear certain types of punishment. There are no statistics available on whether physical or psychological punishment is more effective in correcting behavior patterns, and there is no evidence as to which may cause the most lasting damage. However, punishment that is fundamentally cruel and retributive will often cause anxiety. The fear of punishment is more likely to develop when parents are unpredictable. If a child is aware of the fact that sometimes his parent may punish him and sometimes may not for exactly the same activity, his sense of insecurity may lead to anxiety about punishment. When a child knows why he is being punished and when he can expect it in a fairly dependable way, he is not likely to develop very much fear of it. It is something to be borne. Some children have worked out a scale of values whereby doing something they want very much to do is worth the punishment they will have to take for it. This is particularly true, I think, with boys. When punishment is equated with God's judgment, it becomes an additional psychological device that is likely to do more harm than good.

The fear of war varies with the tensions in the international scene. Because of the increased possibility of thermo-nuclear destruction and our children's growing awareness of the dangers of both direct hits and nuclear fallout, there may be an underlying anxiety about which they feel completely hopeless. Parents may unwillingly contribute to the heightening of this anxiety by virtue of their own knowledge of the danger we are in, or they may share with their children a combination of courageous faith and genuine fatalism about what might happen. It seems to me that in all of these cases where children's fears and anxieties are at stake, the fundamental attitudes of the parents, not simple words of reassurance, are communicated.

76. *Nine-year-old Bobby has a Jewish schoolmate with whom he discusses many things, including religion. As a result of their discussions, Bobby asks his parents what he should believe about the person and nature of Jesus, whom the Jewish child believes (by virtue of his parents' opinion) to have been a fanatic Jew. What can the parents say?*

Questions of this sort, which offer the opportunity for appreciation of other points of view and comparison with one's own, provide our greatest opportunities for teaching. Here is a Jewish boy whose concept of Jesus is different from that of the Christian.

With a nine-year-old boy, it is possible to start with whatever knowledge he has of the Old Testament, which is the Jews' Bible. To recognize this common bond between the Jew and the Christian in our common Old Testament faith is most important. The Jew and the Christian are distinguished from the rest of the world by their historical orientation. Both the Jew and the Christian believe that God is Lord of history and that he intends to redeem the world through sending a Messiah.

This is the expectation toward which the Old Testament points. The Jewish boy, however, accepts the Law of the Old Testament as binding, and therefore maintains certain dietary and ritual rules in his own home which Christians have discarded. Pope Pius once said, "Spiritually we are Semites."

Because the Jew regards the Old Testament as his Bible and expects a Messiah still to come, he rejects the Christian claim that Jesus was the Messiah. The little Jewish boy is quite right in reminding his Christian friend that Jesus was a Jew. Jesus was a son of the covenant and remained a loyal member of the Jewish community until his death. All of the twelve disciples were Jews. After the resurrection, the disciples were finally completely convinced that this Jesus, this great and beloved teacher and prophet, was the Messiah. He had risen from the dead, and this event proved it. The earliest Christians were Jewish converts and continued many of their Jewish practices, including circumcision, until Paul was able to convince the Jerusalem church that his mission to the non-Jews was legitimate and could be worked out with baptism as the means of initiation into the Christian community without circumcision. It was at this point that the Jewish dietary and ritual laws dropped out of Christian practice.

If the parents wish to help their boy, they need to know at least this much about Jewish-Christian relations in the early days. Then they can interpret their information to their child in terms of his own questions and concerns.

Today's Jews agree with Joseph Klausner that Jesus was "a great teacher of morality and an artist in parable. . . . In his ethical code there is a sublimity, distinctiveness and originality in form unparalleled in any other Hebrew ethical code; neither is there any parallel to the remarkable art of his parables."[2]

The Christian accepts this view of Jesus, and therefore the Jew and the Christian are close together in their religious world-views. The differences are real, and they should not be glossed over. But the Jew has given the Christian his heritage, and they belong to the same religious family. This closeness forged what we call our Jewish-Christian heritage in Western civilization.

77. *Arising out of this same context is the question of what nine-year-old Bobby's attitude should be toward his erstwhile Jewish friend, who differs so radically on a point of vital issue. Bobby's parents are uneasily aware that anti-Semitism is wrong, but they are concerned lest the friendship become too close. What attitude is proper and what should be the limitations of the friendship?*

Will Herberg, in his book *Protestant-Catholic-Jew*, has made it clear that in order to be a respectable American, one must belong to one of these three religious communities. There is no reason, on Christian grounds, why a Jew and a Christian cannot be friends. Because Jesus was a Jew, anti-Semitism is anti-Christ. Karl Barth, the great Swiss-German theologian, has said that anti-Semitism is a denial of Christ's resurrection. One may choose to be a friend of a Jew, of another Christian, or of a non-member of the Jewish-Christian community, but this is a matter of personal choice, not of rules and regulations. We all have the right to pick our friends, and parents may help their children choose according to any number of ground rules set up in the home.

If the Jewish boy and the Christian boy have enough interests in common to develop a friendship, the parents should be very careful about trying to limit this friendship or breaking it up, for in doing so they may inculcate feelings of anti-Semitism. On the other hand, they have the right to make suggestions in terms of social, moral, and personality factors, including religion.

78. *Thirteen-year-old Roger and his friend are discussing purgatory. They decide that there is no such place, but are unsure about the existence of a future life. What should Roger's father tell him about immortality and resurrection?*

What happens after death is a problem facing all of us. The New Testament is reticent about any details concerning a future life. It uses various words to describe it: "immortality," "resurrection," "eternal life." Immortality, derived from Greek thinking, expresses the continuance of the spirit or the soul in a life to come. The emphasis is on the death of the body and the continuance of the soul or spirit. Resurrection speaks of being dead completely and coming to life again. This is the manner of thinking inherited by the Jews from the Persians and taken over into the New Testament. In its crudest form, it is a resurrection of the physical body, of the flesh, but as interpreted by Paul, it emphasizes the fact that God gives everlasting life to those who die in faith, and Paul explicitly makes clear that this is not a resurrection of flesh and blood. Eternal life, a phrase used primarily by the author of the Fourth Gospel, indicates a quality of life that is timeless; and it can be entered into now. We already have eternal life because we have belief in Jesus Christ as Lord. These distinctions are important because they show how great the variety is even in the New Testament.

Paul's view in his letter to the Corinthians has been one of the standard descriptions of life after death. He points out by analogy that the seed must die in order to live. In the same way, the body that dies is decayed, and yet what is risen is free from decay. Therefore, he makes a distinction between the physical body which can be corrupted and a spiritual body which rises from the dead. Flesh and blood cannot share in the kingdom of God; what is perishable cannot put on what is imperishable; what is mortal cannot put on immortality; and death is swallowed up in victory. (See I Cor. 15:35–58)

This kind of thinking does not tell us whether there is any purgatory or not. Long ago, in considering God's judgment on men at the time of death, it was felt that most men do not deserve to have either continued relations with God on the one hand or continued separation from him on the other. Most men were believed to be somewhere in the middle, and thus the idea of purgatory as a place where one works out compensations for his sins developed. This provides a neater form of justice, but is pure speculation. In fact, all thinking about heaven and hell is pure speculation and is a reflection of man's idea of God's justice and love.

The best we can say to Roger is that we have very little knowledge about the future life except the hope and assurance that God will give us eternal life. We cannot prove it. Heaven can be described most simply as being in the presence of God and in the right relationship with him, and Hell can be described as being separated from God, being dead to God. Paul asserts this in ringing terms in his letter to the Romans: "If God is for us, who can be against us? For I am convinced that neither death nor life, nor angels nor their hierarchies, nor the present nor the future, nor any supernatural forces either of height or depth will be able to separate us from the love God has shown in Christ Jesus our Lord!" (Romans 8:31, 38–39, P)

79. *Fifteen-year-old Mary is pregnant. Her parents are terribly chagrined and on the point of disowning her. The family doctor has been helpful in taking care of physical and social complications, but is deeply concerned about the parents' attitude. How can the pastor help them through counseling?*

We need to start where Mary is. This is not the time to make recriminations about her past actions, or for the parents or Mary to blame themselves. At this point, there is a situation to be faced immediately in terms of the resources of the Christian faith. Both the parents and Mary are called upon to analyze their attitudes toward each other and also toward the father of the child. This means a re-examination of one's purpose in life and ultimately a development of plans for the future.

In this case, the parents decided to go to the pastor for counseling. His task, it seems to me, is to help them accept the fact that Mary needs their support, understanding, and love. This they may be unable or unwilling to offer. They may be too concerned about what the neighbors or relatives will think of them as parents. It is vitally important, however, for them to understand and accept their own responsibility for the situation Mary is in. It may be that the pregnancy is the result of a moment of weakness on Mary's part, but it is more likely that the parents somehow have failed to provide the understanding and the love that would give Mary the strength to resist the temptation to engage in sexual intercourse. A pastor must help them see clearly what the situation is, their degree of involvement, and their responsibility. Even if Mary's act is outright rebellion, they still have no right to disown her. Mary has the right to return as a prodigal and be received as a daughter in the home. This is easy to say, but may be impossible for the parents to accept emotionally. If this is so, a process of counseling is needed which is beyond the scope of this book.

If the parents can be convinced that Mary needs their support, love, and understanding, then the arrangements made by the family doctor (with Mary's consent and that of the father of the child) can be worked out co-operatively. There are many possible solutions at this point, depending upon the factors in the case: Mary may decide to give up the child for adoption; or it may seem wiser for her to marry the father and keep the child; in a very rare case, the parents may decide to have Mary return to them and bring up the child in their own home.

80. *What books are most helpful for our children when they seek answers to their questions about religion?*

The following books have been carefully selected according to age and are described briefly:

For very little children (younger than six) there is a series of small volumes called Little–Big Books on the Bible, one of the best being *The Good Friends* by Gordon Stowell (Waco, Texas: Word Books, 1971). The simple stories and line drawings appeal to most children between two-and-a-half and five years of age. *Prayer for a Child* by Rachel Field (New York: Macmillan, 1973), *Prayer for Little Things* by Eleanor Farjeon (Boston: Houghton, Mifflin), and *Prayers and Graces for a Small Child* by Mary Alice Jones (Chicago: Rand Mc-

Nally, 1957) have been around a long time and have continued value.

For children six through eight, there is a series of Arch Books that can be used in a variety of ways at home and in Sunday school. A typical one is *The Boy Who Saved His Family* by Alyce Bergey (St. Louis: Concordia, 1966). A very popular book with parents and children alike is *The Christ Child* by Maude and Miska Petersham (Garden City, Doubleday, 1931). The series of books by Mary Alice Jones for this age group has been updated with new pictures in some cases: *Tell Me about God, Tell Me about Jesus, Tell Me about the Bible, Tell Me about Prayer, Tell Me about Christmas, Tell Me about Heaven, His Name Was Jesus* (all published in Chicago by Rand McNally).

The problem of death can be faced by helping children with *Talking about Death* by Earl A. Grollman (Boston: Beacon Press, 1970), or *My Grandpa Died Today* by Joan Fassler (New York: Behavioral Publications, 1971). For understanding the handicapped, try *Howie Helps Himself* by Joan Fassler (Chicago: Albert Whitman and Co., 1975).

For children aged nine through eleven, Walter Russell Bowie's *The Bible Story for Boys and Girls* (Nashville: Abingdon, 1951, 1952) retells the stories of both the Old and New Testaments in two volumes. An unusual Christmas book, for both this age and older, is *The Bethlehem Inn* by Frederick M. Meek (Philadelphia: Westminster, 1972), with its imaginative reconstruction of the events surrounding Jesus' birth. Children have long found value in two classics, *Charlotte's Web* by E. B. White (New York: Dell, 1973), and *The Little Prince* by Antoine de Saint Exupéry (New York: Harcourt Brace Jovanovich, 1968). A mystery story is combined with a biblical story in both *Travelling the Way* by McGowan and Harrison, for ages ten and eleven, and *Young Rebels,* by Ernest Harrison, for ages twelve and up (Toronto: Anglican Book Centre, 1966). *One God: The Ways We Worship Him* by

Florence Mary Fitch (New York: Lothrop, Lee & Sheperd, 1944), with its pictures and text illustrating the Jewish, Roman Catholic, and Protestant customs of worship, is a most important book for all children of this age and older. The companion volume, *Their Search for God: Ways of Worship in the Orient* (Lothrop, 1947), takes the reader into the world beyond Christianity and provides a basis for contrast and reflection. One of the best ways into Bible stories is through the comics when they are well done. *Picture Stories from the Bible* (New York: Ktav, 1971) is a black and white reprint of some color comics of 1943 and covers some dramatic Old Testament stories.

On the junior high level, Alvin N. Rogness has written a book that focuses on a key question for children at about the eighth-grade level: *Youth Asks, Why Bother about God?* (Nashville: Thomas Nelson, 1965). A theological word book with some key explanations is available in *More than Words* (New York: Seabury, 1955, 1958). *Love and Sex in Plain Language* by Eric W. Johnson (Philadelphia: Lippincott, 1974) has information on the junior high level. Chad Walsh has provided a story of two teenagers facing the question of confirmation in *Knock and Enter* (New York: Morehouse-Barlow, 1953). Teenagers should read one of the modern translations of the Bible rather than stories from the Bible retold.

For young people aged fourteen and up, there is a wealth of material. The Youth Forum Series has over twenty volumes, including *Youth Considers "Do-It-Yourself" Religion* by Martin Marty, *Youth Considers Personal Moods* by Reuel L. Howe, *Youth Considers Parents as People* by Randolph C. Miller, *Prayer—Who Needs It?* by Annette Walters, and *Science and Faith—Twin Mysteries* by William G. Pollard (all published in Nashville by Thomas Nelson). Richard Hettlinger's *Growing Up with Sex* (New York: Seabury, 1971) is sound and suitable for both junior and senior high. John Coburn's *Anne and the Sand Dobbies* (New York: Seabury, 1964) is a story interpreting death that will help children and adults. A good way into understanding the Bible is Robert McAfee Brown's classic *The Bible Speaks to You* (Philadelphia: Westminster, 1955). Groups of adults or teenagers will find two books helpful for understanding current problems: *Bias and the Pious* by James E. Dittes (Minneapolis: Augsburg, 1973) deals with the relationship between prejudice and religion; *Bridging the Gap* by Merton P. Strommen (Minneapolis: Augsburg, 1973) deals with the problem of alienation from the church and how to overcome it.

CHAPTER IX

Parents' Religious Attitudes

81. What does the Bible have to offer other than history?

It is possible to read the Bible in a number of different ways. In the first place it is great literature, and the King James' Version is unsurpassed as English literature. In the second place it is good history. Although there is much in the Bible that is not historical, whenever the Bible has been compared with other historical sources and checked by archeological excavations, it turns out to be nearer the truth than the other sources. Third, we have already indicated that the Bible can be looked at as a record of God's acts in history, a drama in which God and men participate. Unless the Bible is more than history, it is valuable only as a record of what people thought a long time ago, and so we need to ask, "How does the Bible fit into the scheme of Christian education?"

A proper use of Scripture, through a sounder Christian education, may make us ready to ask the right questions, prepare us to seek the Lord while he may be found, and incorporate us into the blessed community of faithful people.

First, we discover that we are like many of the characters portrayed in Scripture. We share the murderous anger of Moses (Exodus 2: 11–15) as well as his service through the Law. We have the same adulterous thoughts as David (11 Samuel 11:2–12:25), without the power to carry them through, and yet we have something of his penitence and courage. We flame with the indignation of an Amos or a Jeremiah, and yet we are satisfied with the empty ceremonial of the priests. We find ourselves reflected in the parsimony of Ananias and Sapphira, who held back some of their donation to the church (Acts 5:1–11). We are disturbed by the rich young ruler who could not give his money to the poor (Luke 18:18–30), and yet, like Simon the magician, we think we can buy our way into the church with our money (Acts 8:14–24). We are so much like the respectable Pharisees that we cannot understand why Jesus called them nasty names (Matthew 23:1–39). Sometimes we think that the respectable elder son got the short end of things when the prodigal returned home (Luke 15:25–32). Yet we rejoice when Jesus threw the money-changers out of the Temple (Luke 19:45–46), and we are glad that we are not like Judas.

Beginning therefore to see our own condition, as we find ourselves separated from God and our fellows, we wonder if we need to be saved, and this leads us to the questions we need to ask.

Second, people in the Bible did not discover how to meet their needs until they sought their Lord. Judas and Peter each denied Christ in his own way, but Judas was destroyed because his betrayal was final, and Peter was saved because he repented of his denial. Judas may have been endowed with more brains than Peter, but Peter, with his big heart, somehow blundered through until he found the answer.

When we are confronted with the real meaning of the Scriptures, we find that we face the same question that Judas and Peter faced: "Is Jesus your Christ?" Judas denied it and Peter accepted it. Thomas doubted it until he had proof; then he cried out, "My Lord and My God!" (John 20:24–29)

Third, when we examine the Scriptures from our youth up, we discover one other factor: the Bible is the book of the church. Within it, the church appears as the community of the Holy Spirit. The men and women of the Bible, so much like ourselves in every way, found in the fellowship of the church the strength to become and to remain loyal followers of Jesus Christ. By God's grace they became new persons, transformed and reborn from above. The lost were found, the lonely were restored to fellowship, and sinners were redeemed. They discovered that God loved them, no matter how unloving they were, and because God loved them they could be saved. They responded to this love by living heroically. They bore witness to their faith; they died as martyrs; they went to the outermost parts of the earth as missionaries; and they lived with each other in such a way that observers said, "Behold how these Christians love one another!"

An early Christian document called *The Address to Diognetus* described the Christians of that period: "For Christians are not distinguished from the rest of mankind in country or speech or customs. For they do not live somewhere in cities of their own or use some distinctive language or practice a peculiar manner of life. They have no learning discovered by the thought and reflection of inquisitive men, nor are they the authors of any human doctrine, like some men. Though they live in Greek and Barbarian cities, as each man's lot is cast, and follow the local customs in dress and food and the rest of their living, their own way of life which they display is wonderful and admittedly strange. . . .

"Like everyone else they marry, they have children, but they do not expose their infants. They set a common table, but not a common bed. They find themselves in the flesh, but they do not live after the flesh. They remain on earth, but they are citizens of heaven. . . . Those who hate them cannot give a reason for their hostility.

"To put it briefly, what the soul is to the body, Christians are to the world. . . . To so high a station God has appointed them, and it is not right for them to refuse it."[1]

82. How can the church help my family to find a secure place in our community?

In *The Address to Diognetus*, quoted in answer to the previous question, there is very little about security for Christians in this world. In another portion of the same address, the writer says Christians "love all men, and are persecuted by all men. . . . They are dishonored, and in their dishonor they are glorified. They are abused, and they are vindicated. . . . When they do good, they are punished as evil doers; when they are punished, they rejoice as though they were being made alive."[2]

The mature Christian finds his security in things other than the goods of this world. The church has been accused of being other-worldly and of offering an other-worldly type of security, and to a great extent it is guilty of this charge. The Book of Job, in the Old Testament, is a example of a way in which a man may lose everything he depends upon in his life—his land, his wealth, and his family—and when all that remains is his own self in relation to God, he is still able to put his trust in God (Job 13:15). Nothing the world could do destroyed Job's faith; this was his ultimate security. Jesus put this clearly when he said, "Do not fear those who kill the body, but cannot kill the soul. Fear him rather who is able to destroy both soul and body in hell" (Matthew 10:28, NEB). The confidence, integrity, and security of those who have faith in God show in their daily living. When we reach the point at which we can say with Jesus, "Be not anxious about tomorrow" (Matthew 6:25; Luke 12:22), then can we find the resources to do all of our own jobs in this world without feelings of insecurity. The ultimate security rests in God, and is reflected in the interpersonal relationships of family life, of friendship, and of the church when it is really a community of the Holy Spirit. Many families and churches do not offer this kind of interpersonal relationship, and in this instance even those who have faith are frustrated.

The promise is stated thus: "All who follow the leading of God's Spirit are God's own sons. Nor are you meant to relapse into the old slavish attitude of fear—you have been adopted into the very family circle of God, and you can say with a full heart, 'Father, my Father.' The Spirit himself endorses our inward conviction that we really are the children of God. Think what that means! If we are his children we share his treasures, and all that Christ claims as his will belong to all of us as well! It is plain to anyone with eyes to see that at the present time all creative life groans in a sort of universal travail. And it is plain, too, that we who have a foretaste of the Spirit are in a state of painful tension, while we wait for that redemption of our bodies which will mean at last that we have attained our full sonship with him. We were saved by this hope, but in our moments of impatience, let us remember that hope always means waiting for something we haven't yet got. But if we hope for something we cannot see, then we must settle down to wait for it in patience" (Romans 8:14–17, 22–24, P).

From the point of view of everyday life, this orientation of the self toward God makes all the difference. It is not something that comes easily; it demands patience. And yet, in the maturity of faith, there is a peace that passes understanding. We arrive at a point where we do not fear what men can do to us. This supreme confidence of the Christian is communicated to those whom he loves, and it produces those powers that help to set right the injustices of our society. The Christian is one who is willing to take a risk for what is right. He is willing to give up his life for his country, for his family—indeed, for whatever is worth while.

83. In doing my duty in the business world, I am sometimes required to do things I don't think are right. Should I feel guilty about this? What is my real duty?

In order to live in the world, it is necessary to make compromises. Although the church has never been more irrelevant than when it is isolated from the world with its own private society, there is a sense in which it *must* stand "over against" the world. This applies to the Christian as well. Thus, in taking part in one's business or in functioning in a community or even in some cases in maintaining the structure of a family, one necessarily faces compromise.

Conscience is the capacity to choose between right and wrong, and its content is provided by education and culture. A

Christian conscience is governed by faith in Christ and by the power to resist temptation.

It is not easy to face the world with "the same attitude Jesus Christ had" (Philippians 2:5 G). The Bible does not give the Christian guidance in specific matters peculiar to the twentieth century. If biblical principles are to be applied, then twentieth-century man needs guidance. He receives some help from the church; but churches differ. In any case, the Christian must make his own decision, knowing that he is not infallible.

Let us assume that a person has an accurate idea of what Christ would want him to do, and that he wants to follow his conscience in his daily living. He may discover a contradiction between certain demands of his job and the concern for persons which stands at the center of the Gospel ethics. A salesman may be working from an advertising folder in which his product is misrepresented, or on a sales program in which prices are adjusted to the customer's resources or gullibility. A teenager faces similar problems if he wants to be an accepted member of a social group.

No one can withdraw from his surroundings without defaulting on other obligations. The only place in which one can express his conscience is the society in which he lives, and in order to stay within that society he must make compromises. The only other solution is to become a hermit.

Decisions concerning social compromise are often more complex than they seem. Our options are almost always between shades of gray. If I, as a doctor, tell the patient the truth, I may hasten his death and therefore be a partner to his demise. If I refuse to tell him what is wrong, he may imagine a condition worse than what is actually the case. If a well-known gossip asks me a direct question, I may do great harm by answering honestly and contributing to the publicity of truths that should remain private. Both the conscientious objector and the soldier face responsibilities far more complex than merely choosing between alternatives of killing and being killed.

The danger of a rigid ethic is nowhere more obvious than

in the church's treatment of divorce and remarriage. An easy divorce is often a way out of a difficult but far from impossible situation, one in which all concerned might be better off if the marriage were made to work. Children suffer from the privation of not having a father or a mother. On the other hand, there are cases where divorce is the only answer for the good of the children and at least for one and perhaps both of the parents. On the question of remarriage after divorce, the churches have been even more rigid, and this has led to much unnecessary suffering. Yet the sanctity of marriage makes a witness against divorce and remarriage necessary. Some compromise becomes necessary, and some communions choose to recognize ecclesiastical annulment; others remarry the innocent party (but how can anyone tell who is "ultimately" innocent?); and others remarry almost anyone. Any law rigidly enforced is too simple to deal in a Christian manner with the complexities of such relationships; and yet even a Christian conscience demands some kind of guidance.

These necessary compromises are often disguised or pushed back into the subconscious. An outstanding layman claimed that Christianity dealt with only personal ethics and had nothing to do with race relations. Ministers have been told to "stick to the Gospel" and not to talk about the ethics of General Motors. A group of young people came to the conclusion that if they wanted dates for a necking party they should turn to a religious group that barred smoking, drinking and card-playing—assuming that the problems of boy-girl relations had not been faced by that particular group.

The Bible tells us that we face every ethical decision as sinners for whom Christ died. In many cases we are powerless to resist temptation even when we know what God's will is. But in many more cases, the situation is so complex that any choice fails to reflect the attitude that Christ had, and we cannot successfully apply the ideals of Christ to the many human relationships and values involved.

This leads to what I have called the ethics of *approximation*.[3]

This, I think, is a stronger and more positive term than "compromise." God is absolute, and his will is perfect, and God expresses his will in history and in cultural situations. The Holy Spirit is God at work in the world and in us. Therefore, God's will becomes relevant to our human situation, and whenever God's will is translated into human terms, it becomes permeated with the relativities of our experience and culture. We do not achieve God's absolute will, but there is a continuum between what man can do and what God requires, and thus we can approximate God's will for us. We stand between the poles of tension expressed in two quotations from Jesus; "You, therefore, must be perfect, as your heavenly Father is perfect" (Matthew 5:48 RSV), and "Why do you call me good? No one is good but God alone" (Luke 18:19 RSV).

In being committed to God's will, we seek to discover all of the possibilities that are open to us. Sometimes we have a simple choice between good and evil, and if we happen to choose the good, we are in danger of falling into the sin of pride. There are some tragic situations in which all we can do is choose the lesser of two evils, as in the case of war. But in many cases the choice is between lesser and greater goods, both of which fall short of the good that God commands. There are times when no compromise is possible. "Here I stand. I can do no other. God help me. Amen," said Martin Luther. We may have to face martyrdom, which may include loss of a job, harmful publicity, a ruined reputation, or death. In this generation, there have been Christians who have suffered, lost jobs, and died because they believed that they must bear witness to the will of God. It may be a young mother taking her children to school in New Orleans, it may be a Bishop facing the Communists, it may be a man who no longer can do his job with a clear conscience. The law of God is higher than the law of country or church, and there are times when men must choose.

Most of us are involved in a culture to which we need to make adjustments. We find ourselves opposed to some aspects of our culture, and yet we know God's purposes are worked out in culture. There is no escape from this tension either for children or adults. In the end, we come to God as sinners, redeemed by the act of God in Christ and not through anything that we do. We face God's judgment with hope, not because we are virtuous, but because we have been redeemed. God loves us, and we have sought to be worthy, and we live in the hope of resurrection unto eternal life.

84. My wife and I would like to find a few nice friends, but we don't know anybody in the neighborhood and nobody ever visits us. Can the church give us programs whereby we might meet people of similar social interests?

Every church tries to do what is asked for in this question. There has been a growing recognition that Christian fellowship is most likely to develop in social groupings of about ten couples or twenty adults all concerned more or less with the same religious issues in their lives. In some cases, recreation and the pleasant use of leisure time are as important in developing this fellowship as is study or a common activity. The Protestant churches are particularly susceptible to this kind of socializing, even on a secular level, because of the freedom of Protestants to attend the church of their choice. Therefore, a church is likely to serve the neighborhood or "like-minded" people from various neighborhoods through satisfying secular interests rather than through sharing a religious outlook as such. This obviously offers a danger in respect to the proclamation of the Gospel and our strong desire that people of all classes and races should be able to worship and work together. But it often happens that people who have much in common are drawn together in and through the churches.

If I were to come into a new community and for purely secular reasons wanted to meet a number of people who might share my outlook, I would seek out the nearest church. If I were to enter a community and wanted to meet a number of people who would share my religious views, again I would seek out the nearest church. If I were merely searching for a church "home" for my children, I would also seek out the nearest church. If for any of these reasons I sought out a church and did not find the answer to my needs, I would not quit, but would keep looking for a church in my area until I found one that met these needs.

We need to remember that God is not concerned primarily with religion but with people. Therefore, people who are seeking the church for almost any reason are likely to find answers to their needs in and through the church; for the church ministers to the whole person in God's world.

85. I want to invest my leisure time in something that really lasts. Where could I do this in the church?

One of the most important developments in Christian thinking today is the ministry of the laity. Many of our congregations are large organizations that need careful administration, and often the most important parts of the administrative job are purely secular. Many ministers have discovered that they are spending over half their time running organizations as business managers. The lay people in the church, with their competence in the business world, can volunteer their leisure time to help keep the organization running well. This is an extremely important part of the laymen's ministry and in some cases it has become a professional ministry.

For example, if a businessman decides that he would like to retire at the age of 60 or 65, but would like to "keep busy" as far as business affairs are concerned, he might very well be appointed the business manager of the church on a fulltime basis. In some instances this would carry a salary; in others it might be a volunteer job—his offering to the church.

If lay people are interested in getting something creative *from* the church rather than in giving *to* the church, there are many study groups, activity groups, and other organizations in the church which could very well take up most of their spare time. While some of these activities are not worth while, others are at the very heart of our understanding of the Christian faith. Many men and women who have free time are finding ways of working in the church through such groups.

86. *Some of our meetings with other people are on a superficial level, as at cocktail parties. Can the church help us discover more genuine kinds of personal relationships?*

A number of social activities in many churches is on the level of a cocktail party. Sometimes the coffee hour after services reaches no deeper level than this. This is not necessarily bad, because only through casual relationships on a superficial level can we hope to make personal contacts that will lead to deeper relationships. Almost any kind of interpersonal relationship begins on the superficial level. Only as we are able to move beyond this stage, through repeated encounters, can we share our deeper and more genuine concerns.

Many organizations of the church are geared to achieve exactly this. Small groups of interested people, limited to about twenty, meet according to neighborhood, vocational group, concern with religious issues, or on some other basis. These people will consider their first impressions, and ultimately, as the gathering becomes an integrated group, they will partake of serious discussions on vital issues. We cannot expect this to happen the first time an organization meets, even if it is a church organization.

When we first attend a new church, the worship, too, may seem to be on a superficial level. We may like or dislike the sermon, or the choir, or the liturgical practices, or the congregation. We may accept our common Christian loyalty in the congregation but do very little about it. Sometimes the worship of our churches never gets deeper than this superficial level, which is why there is great dissatisfaction with the worship of some congregations. But where there is genuine interpersonal concern within the parish, the worship takes on a reality that reflects the interpersonal meetings among the effective membership of the congregation.

87. My wife has a college degree, and because she spends most of her time in the house and with the children, she feels that she is neglecting her best capacities. Can the church help her feel that she is fulfilled by caring for her family?

Many college-educated mothers who tend to lose their intellectual curiosity because of their responsibilities in the home can be helped to realize that their capacities are fully involved in the responsibilities of motherhood. When they realize that the way in which they feed, train, and inspire their children, care for their families, and maintain their homes carries out a Christian vocation, they will discover that this is God's work in the world and a true ministry of the Gospel.

When we consider Christian vocations, measuring one's work in respect to the needs of others and the welfare of the world (as well as one's own aptitudes), we must recognize motherhood as one of the most important. It is true that there is a great deal of drudgery in running a home; yet society's judgment of mothers is that they belong at the top of the scale. Motherhood is a high calling. A woman's evaluation of her role, depending on her own attitude, makes the chief difference. In home life, relationships are built around hard work, and companionship undergirds them. There is love to provide a united front against difficulty. Building a family is a Christian vocation. A mother is called of God to her task, and therefore even the most menial chore takes on dignity and sanctity.

In a very real sense, the mother is the center of a Christian home. Her vocation is a full-time occupation.

There are mothers who, out of a mistaken sense of duty, turn their lives into sheer drudgery. They become the slaves of their children and forget that their vocation is a dual one. They are to be mothers to their children but also wives to their husbands. In order to be a companion to a husband, a woman needs to be alert to the world in which he lives, to share his interests, and to have interests of her own in which he can share. The problem to be solved, then, is not how to escape the limitations of motherhood but how to make sure that a woman's horizons are inclusive enough.

A mother needs to work herself out of a job, so that the children will be free to leave the home. A wife needs to stay on the job, because she never ceases to be a wife to her husband. When a woman realizes that her vocation as wife actually outranks her vocation as mother, she will be able to view her work in the proper perspective. It is a matter of simple statistics. If a couple expect to live together for approximately fifty years, less than twenty-five of these years will be spent in rearing children. At the end of that time, if husband and wife have not maintained their primary vocation as lovers and companions, there will be nothing but a vacuum when the children leave home. Furthermore, in order to maintain this companionship both husband and wife need to keep growing as individual human beings.

The church can contribute to the developing wholeness of a woman by helping her at three levels of her growth: first, by helping her to become a mother and to fulfill her vocation; second, by helping her to see that her position as wife will outlast her position as mother and will provide satisfactions that are otherwise impossible; third, by bringing out the potentialities in every woman to accept the claim of God upon her in whatever ways are open. Study groups, activities, and genuine challenges are essential to an adequate church program for women. It is important for the wife and mother to be part of a group that includes the husband and father. Clubs for couples can be enriching to people's lives.

88. What do parents have to look forward to after their children have left home?

Anne Proctor, an English mother of seven, has given this question its true perspective in her book *Background to Marriage,* in which she writes: "We are lovers before we are parents. Our children are the fruit of our love as much as the fruit of our bodies. This is a fact of family life which we should never forget during those years when we concentrate on bringing up our children. Children are an incident in married life, a terribly important incident which needs all the attention and responsibility of which we are capable, but an incident no less. This is especially true today when families are small and the period of concentration is comparatively short for many couples. If our married life is a success, we will be lovers still when our work as parents is over."[4]

Parents who have fulfilled their parental responsibilities and who joyfully receive their children back as adults are maintaining their relationship as husband and wife, but beyond this is the significance of God's presence in their relationship, going back to the beginning of their married life.

We return to the fact that we have each other. Marriage is always a relationship between two limited and sinful human beings. If I can learn to accept my wife as she is, not trying to reform her but only to love her and live with her, if I can ask her to forgive me for my faults and can bring myself to forgive her whether she asks me to or not, we have a basis for a continuing and successful marriage.

The "vow and covenant" of the marriage service is a pledge of faithfulness which undergirds and strengthens the love because it is part of it. I can trust this person who loves me because this love is based on an act of will, on our mutual interest, and on our desire to possess and to be possessed. When such a combination is sound, the world cannot destroy it. In *I and Thou*, Martin Buber emphasizes the importance of knowing the other person *as a person*. I treat you as a "thou" when you are an end in yourself, a person with rights, privileges, and freedom to be what you are. I treat you as an "it" when I use you for my own ends, making you a means, a thing, to be manipulated. Love sees the beloved as a whole person, with a secret potential to become what only the lover can see. My wife is not just a sex symbol, not just a mother, not just one who runs our house. She is these things, but she is also a total person, and I place her well-being first in all my decisions.

89. *What are some of the important books for parents?*

Parents have a great deal at stake in their choice of books providing information about their responsibility in the field of religion. One of the most helpful of these, especially for parents with some understanding of Freud, is *Your Growing Child and Religion* by Roy W. Lee (New York: Macmillan, 1963). A book with a wide variety of source material and research reports is *Your Child and Religion* by Johanna Klink (Atlanta: John Knox, 1973). Three books by Reuel L. Howe are of primary importance for an overview as well as specific suggestions: *Man's Need and God's Action* (New York: Seabury, 1953), which is especially helpful with the interpretation of relationships from a religious perspective and includes a discussion of infant baptism; *The Creative Years* (New York: Seabury, 1959) is concerned with parents in middle age and their relationships to each other and to their teenagers; *Herein Is Love* (Valley Forge: Judson, 1961) interprets love in terms of family life. J. C. Wynn's *Christian Parents Face Family Problems* (Philadelphia: Westminster, 1955) shows how perennial most family crises are.

A wonderful new book, tying in children's development with all kinds of celebrations, is *Children of Joy: Raising Your Own Home Grown Christians* by David and Elizabeth Gray and their children, Lisa and Hunter (Brooklyn: Reader Press, 1975).

A number of books now provide some research information on religious development. Among some of the best of these are *Introducing Young Children to Jesus* by Violet Madge (New York: Morehouse-Barlow, 1971), which grew out of her earlier research in *Children in Search of Meaning* (New York: Morehouse-Barlow, 1966). Ronald Goldman's research, based on Piaget's categories, has led to two volumes: *Religious Thinking from Childhood to Adolescence* (New York: Seabury, 1968), which relates his research findings, and *Readiness for Religion* (New York: Seabury, 1970), which makes suggestions for curriculum and life-theme approaches to religious knowledge. The current interest in giving Holy Communion to children is dealt with by Urban T. Holmes in *Young Children and the Eucharist* (New York: Seabury, 1972). Ethel M. Smither, in *Children and the Bible* (Nashville: Abingdon, 1960), suggests what children should read or hear at various ages. John Wren-Lewis, in *What Shall We Tell Our Children?* (London: Constable, 1971), suggests a rather skeptical approach to religious questions. *Explaining Death to Children*, edited by Earl A. Grollman (Boston: Beacon Press, 1969), suggests a variety of answers to youngsters' queries, as does my *Live Until You Die* (Philadelphia: Pilgrim, 1973).

If you are concerned with moral development, Norman and Sheila Williams, in *The Moral Development of Children* (Hamden, Conn: Shoe String Press, 1971), provide suggestions based on their research in Great Britain. The impact of TV is brought out sharply by Nat Rutstein in *Go Watch TV* (New York: Sheed & Ward, 1974).

Merton Strommen has focused on the way youth sees itself in *Five Cries of Youth* (New York: Harper and Row, 1974). Sara Little suggests ways in which the church can include youth as full participants, in *Youth, World, and Church* (Atlanta: John Knox, 1968). *We Were Never Their Age*, by James DiGiacomo and Edward Wakin (New York: Holt, Rinehart, and Winston, 1972), deals with parental frustration in trying to understand teenagers.

Some parents will want to read more widely. They could not do better than go back over 100 years to *Christian Nurture*, by Horace Bushnell (New Haven: Yale University Press, 1966). For the current scene, an overall picture is given in *Colloquy on Christian Education* edited by John Westerhoff III (Philadelphia: Pilgrim, 1972). In order to keep up to date, more technically minded readers will enjoy reading *Religious Education*, a bimonthly multifaith professional journal (409 Prospect St., New Haven, Conn. 06510). To gain some grasp of current theological trends, my *The American Spirit of Theology* (Philadelphia: Pilgrim, 1974) or *The New Consciousness in Science and Religion*, by Harold K. Schilling (Philadelphia: Pilgrim, 1973), are technical and helpful.

Parents will want to deepen their own sense of the meaning of life. Devotional books such as *Creative Brooding*, edited by Robert Raines (New York: Macmillan, 1966) will help some people. Others will be helped by a study of *Prayer in a Secular World* by Leroy T. Howe (Philadelphia: Pilgrim, 1973) or *The Courage to Be* by Paul Tillich (New Haven: Yale University Press, 1952). Parents in the midst of frustration and difficulties may find my *Living with Anxiety* (Philadelphia: Pilgrim, 1971) a book for ready reference. If biography is uplifting, try James W. McClendon's *Biography as Theology* (Nashville: Abingdon, 1974).

Finally there is singing. The best book to introduce children to hymn singing is *Sing for Joy*, compiled and edited by Norman and Margaret Mealy (New York: Seabury, 1961), which lists what hymns and refrains can be sung at various ages. *The Whole World Singing*, compiled by Edith Lovell Thomas (New York: Friendship Press, 1950), is another good source.

Notes

CHAPTER I

1. Paul Tillich, *Shaking the Foundations* (New York: Charles Scribner's Sons; 1948), p. 162.
2. Reuel L. Howe, *Herein Is Love* (Philadelphia: Judson Press; 1961), pp. 65–81.
3. Ernest M. Ligon, *Dimensions of Character* (New York: The Macmillan Co.; 1956).

CHAPTER II

1. This approach to the Bible is described in detail and applied to all the age groups in my *Biblical Theology and Christian Education* (New York: Charles Scribner's Sons; 1956).
2. Thomas van B. Barrett, *The Christian Family* (New York: Morehouse-Barlow Co., Inc.; 1958), p. 78.

CHAPTER III

1. Gibson Winter, *Love and Conflict* (Garden City, N.Y.: Doubleday & Company, Inc. [Dolphin Book]; 1958), pp. 71–95.
2. *Ibid.*, pp. 97–119.
3. Howe, *op. cit.*, pp. 66–67.
4. See Basil A. Yeaxlee, *Religion and the Growing Mind* (Greenwich: The Seabury Press, Inc.; 1952), pp. 57–58.
5. *Ibid.*, p. 145.
6. Horace Bushnell, *Christian Nurture* (New Haven: Yale University Press; 1948 ed.), p. 76.
7. *Ibid.*, p. 99.

CHAPTER IV

1. See R. B. Dierenfield, "The Extent of Religious Influence in American Public Schools," *Religious Education*, May–June 1961, pp. 173–79.
2. See Miller M. Cragon, Jr., "The Religious Influence of a Parochial School," *Religious Education*, May–June 1961, pp. 180–84.
3. See Kenneth E. Hyde, "The Religious Concepts of Adolescents," *Religious Education*, September–October 1961, pp. 329–34; also, my *Christian Nurture and the Church*, (New York: Charles Scribner's Sons; 1961), pp. 1–4.
4. See John B. McDowell, *The Development of the Idea of God in the Catholic Child* (Washington: The Catholic University of America Press; 1952), p. 77.

CHAPTER V

1. Bushnell, *op. cit.*, pp. 34–35.
2. See my *Biblical Theology and Christian Education, op. cit.*
3. See my *Christian Nurture and the Church, op. cit.*, Chap. 1.

CHAPTER VI

1. See my *Education for Christian Living* (Englewood Cliffs, N.J.: Prentice-Hall, Inc.; 1956), pp. 308–9.
2. Marjorie Reeves, *Growing Up in a Modern Society* (London: University of London Press; 1952).

CHAPTER VII

1. *The Hymnal* (New York: Church Pension Fund; 1940, 1943), No. 504.
2. D. S. Bailey, *The Mystery of Love and Marriage* (New York: Harper & Brothers; 1953), p. 52.

Chapter VIII

1. Mary Alice Jones, *Tell Me about God* (Chicago: Rand McNally & Co.; 1943) p. 43; see my *The Clue to Christian Education* (New York: Charles Scribner's Sons; 1950), p. 48.
2. Joseph Klausner, *Jesus of Nazareth* (New York: The Macmillan Co.; 1925), p. 414.

Chapter IX

1. *The Address to Diognetus*, 5:1-4, 6-9, 17; 6:1, 10. In *The Apostolic Fathers*, translated by Edgar J. Goodspeed (New York: Harper & Brothers; 1950), pp. 278-79.
2. *Ibid.*, p. 278.
3. See my *The Clue to Christian Education* (New York: Charles Scribner's Sons; 1950), pp. 138-45.
4. Anne Proctor, *Background to Marriage* (New York: Longmans, Green & Co., Inc.; 1953), p. 62.

Index